LIST OF CONTENTS

Cover: Salvaged Sherman DD Tank restored
and dedicated as a War Memorial
at Courseulles, Normandy

3

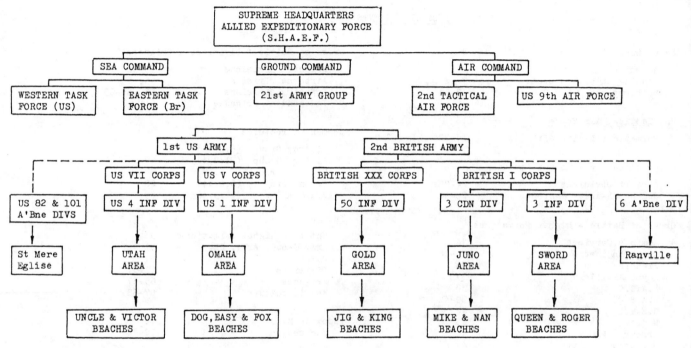

SUPREME HEADQUARTERS
ALLIED EXPEDITIONARY FORCE
(S.H.A.E.F.)

SEA COMMAND — GROUND COMMAND — AIR COMMAND

WESTERN TASK FORCE (US) — EASTERN TASK FORCE (Br)

21st ARMY GROUP

2nd TACTICAL AIR FORCE — US 9th AIR FORCE

1st US ARMY — 2nd BRITISH ARMY

US VII CORPS — US V CORPS — BRITISH XXX CORPS — BRITISH I CORPS

US 82 & 101 A'Bne DIVS — US 4 INF DIV — US 1 INF DIV — 50 INF DIV — 3 CDN DIV — 3 INF DIV — 6 A'Bne DIV

St Mere Eglise — UTAH AREA — OMAHA AREA — GOLD AREA — JUNO AREA — SWORD AREA — Ranville

UNCLE & VICTOR BEACHES — DOG, EASY & FOX BEACHES — JIG & KING BEACHES — MIKE & NAN BEACHES — QUEEN & ROGER BEACHES

COMMAND STRUCTURE - ALLIED EXPEDITIONARY FORCE - 6th JUNE 1944

21st ARMY GROUP

ORDER OF BATTLE

Compiled and published by:-

Mr. MALCOLM A. BELLIS
10 WHITE HART LANE
WISTASTON, CREWE
CHESHIRE, CW2 8EX
ENGLAND

1

INTRODUCTION

21st Army Group, comprising British 2nd Army and Canadian 1st Army, was formed in the United Kingdom in September 1943. It carried out the invasion of Europe in June 1944 (with 1st U.S. Army under command) and fought in Northern France, the Low Countries and Northern Germany, it's Commander accepting the surrender of the German Army at Luneburg Heath on 6th June 1945. At various times the 21st Army Group also had under command U.S. 1st, 3rd and 9th Armies and 1st Allied Airborne Army.

In August 1945, H.Q. 21st Army Group became H.Q. British Army on the Rhine (B.A.O.R), retaining post-war military command in the British Zone of Occupied Germany. In later years, it continued to be present in West Germany as part of N.A.T.O. forces in Europe, and as such is still in existance today.

During the Normandy invasion, 21st Army Group was supported by a total of 6,939 ships and craft in some 47 convoys. Subsequantly, merchant ships supplied all logistic support for the forces in Normandy and the Low Countries, in addition to supplies for use by the civil population. Only a few of the ships and craft used have been listed in this volume, these being considered to be most closely involved with land engagements.

During the Landings, 2nd Tactical Air Force ensured command of the air, covering an area fifteen miles to sea to five miles inland of the Beaches. Subsequently, ground attack aircraft such as the rocket-firing Typhoons were employed against enemy strongholds and lines of communication and for aerial reconnaissance. The squadrons and types of aircraft under command of 2nd Tactical Air Force have been listed, together with the units employed in the air assaults of Normandy, Arnhem and the Rhine.

Even after nearly fifty years, the size and complexity of the Group, and the organisation it required, is astonishing. In this small publication it has only been possible to document a representative sample of each arm of service within Army Group and Army Troops. Divisions and Brigades have been documented in more detail together with dates of service.

During research for this book, material appertaining to vehicle markings and establishment/organisation of units under command of 21st Army Group has been retained, and it is intended that this will be fully documented and published as a companion volume at a future date.

Malcolm A. Bellis   ©1991

SEABORNE SUPPORT

EASTERN TASK FORCE - INVASION PHASE - 6th JUNE 1944

TASK FORCE COMMAND Cruiser HMS Scylla (8x 4.5in) Flagship, Cruiser HMS Sirius (10x 5.25in), Battleship HMS Rodney (9x 16in, 12x 6in). Other flagships thus *

BOMBARDING FORCE 'K' (GOLD)

Cruisers: HMS Orion, HMS Ajax (8x 6in), HMS Emerald (7x 6in), HMS Argonaut (10x 5.25in)*,
Gunboats: HNMS Flores (Dutch)(3x 5.9in)
Destroyers: HMS Grenville, HMS Jerius, HMS Ulster, HMS Ulysses, HMS Undine, HMS Undaunted, HMS Ursa, HMS Urania, HMS Urchin (all 4x or 8x 4.7in), HMS Cattistock, HMS Pytchley, ORP Krakowiak (Polish) (all 4x or 6x 4in)

BOMBARDING FORCE 'E' (JUNO)

Cruisers: HMS Belfast (12x 6in)*, HMS Diadem (8x 5.25in)
Destroyers: HMS Faulknor, HMS Fury, HMS Kempenfeldt, HMS Venus, HMS Vigilant, HMCS Algonquin, HMCS Sioux (all 4x or 8x 4.7in), HMS Bleasdale, HMS Stevenstone, HNMS Glaisdale (Norwegian), FFS La Combattante (all 4x or 6x 4in)

BOMBARDING FORCE 'D' (SWORD)

Battleships: HMS Warspite (4x 15in, 8x 6in), HMS Ramillies (4x 15in, 12x 6in)
Monitors: HMS Roberts (2x 15in)
Cruisers: HMS Mauritius (12x 6in)*, HMS Arethusa (6x 6in), HMS Frobisher (7x 7.5in), HMS Danae (5x 6in), ORP Dragon (Polish)(6x 6in)
Destroyers: HMS Kelvin, HMS Saumarez, HMS Scorpion, HMS Scourge, HMS Swift, HMS Serapis, HMS Virago, HMS Verulum, HNMS Stord (Norwegian), HNMS Svenner (Norwegian), (all 4x or 8x 4.7in), HMS Middleton, HMS Eglinton (4x or 6x 4in)

ASSAULT FORCE COMMAND HMS Bulolo (GOLD), HMS Hilary (JUNO), HMS Largs (SWORD)

NAVAL FORCE 'T' - SCHELDT ESTUARY - OCTOBER 1944

HMS Kingsmill (Frigate)*, HMS Warspite (Battleship), HMS Roberts (Monitor)
HMS Erebus (Monitor)

H.M.S. BELFAST MOORED AT TOWER BRIDGE, LONDON

EASTERN TASK FORCE - LANDING SHIPS & CRAFT

LANDING SHIPS	DESCRIPTION	No. VESSELS
Landing Ship Infantry	Mainly converted merchant ships & ferries of various tonnage, e.g.	37
	4000 tons : 850 troops, 6 Landing Craft Assault, 150 tons cargo.	
	13000 tons: 700 troops, 500 crew, 24 Landing Craft Assault, 3 Landing Craft Mechanised	
Landing Ship Tank	Specially designed sea-going vessels	130
Support Ships	Landing Ship Emergency Repair	2
	Landing Ship (Dock)	1

MAJOR LANDING CRAFT (Cross-Channel under own power)

Landing Craft Infantry (Large)	Bow ramp, 200 troops per craft, 15 knots	116
Landing Craft Infantry (Small)	100 troops per craft, wooden construction	39 (8)
Landing Craft Tank	Specially designed sea-going vessels	487 (14?)
Landing Craft Gun (Large)	2x 4.7in guns, 2-7 Oerlikon 20mm	16 (6)
Landing Craft Gun (Medium)	2x 17 pdr high-velocity guns (in turrets)	- (2)
Landing Craft Tank (Rocket)	800-1000x 5in HE Rocket Projectiles	22 (5)
Landing Craft (Flak)	4x 2pdr, 8x Oerlikon 20mm or 8x 2pdr, 4x Oerlikon 20mm	18 (5)
Landing Craft Assault (Hedgerow)	24x 60 lb spigot bombs	45
Landing Craft Support (Large)	1x 2pdr/6pdr tank turret, 2x Oerlikon 20mm 2x .5cal MGs, 1x 4in Smoke Mortar	14
Landing Craft Support (Medium)	2x .5cal MGs, 1x 4in Smoke Mortar	24
Landing Craft Tank (Support)	Vehicles loaded were intended to use their armament whilst still at sea. Total load carried by all vessels was 80x 90mm Centaurs, 240x 25pdr/105mm SP Field Guns. Three craft were loaded with 17pdr HV Guns.	103

Note; nos in brackets for Scheldt Ops

EASTERN TASK FORCE - MINOR LANDING CRAFT & FERRIES

MINOR LANDING CRAFT (embarked on sea-going ships)   No Vessels

Landing Craft Assault (LCA)   wooden hull, carried on ships davitts,
                                       36 troops or 10 tons cargo

Landing Craft (Vehicle & Personnel)   US version of Landing Craft Assault,   (408 total)
                                       36 troops or 3-ton truck

Landing Craft (Personnel)   Earlier version of above without the
                                       provision for vehicle. Carried 36 troops
                                       (US vessels) or 25 troops (RN vessels)

Landing Craft (Mechanised)   Unladen weight 22 tons, vehicle load 18 tons,
                                       carried on heavy derick of merchant ships.

ROYAL MARINE UNITS

'E' Squadron	flotillas 605,606,607,609,654,698	total 76 Landing Craft Mechanised
'B' Squadron	flotillas 805,806,807,808,809	total 80 Landing Craft Mechanised
Independent	flotillas 557,700,706	total 40 Landing Craft Personnel

SHIP TO SHORE FERRIES

Landing Ferry - Rhino   steel pontoons, detatchable propulsion
                                 section. Largest vessels of 400 tons,
                                 (175ft x 45ft)   41

Landing Barges   Landing Barge Vehicle   120

                                 Landing Barge Flak   15

                                 Landing Barge - Ancilliary Services   115

LANDING SHIP TANK MK II

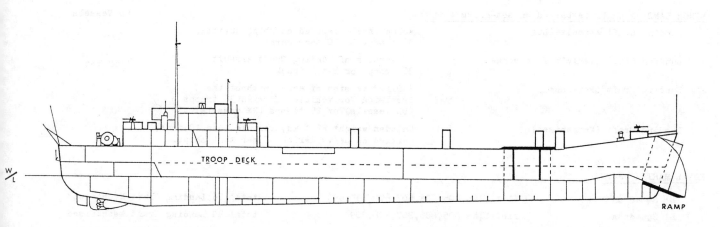

TROOP DECK

W/L

RAMP

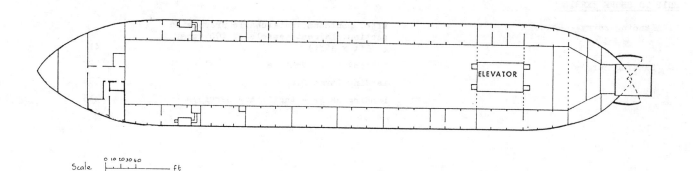

ELEVATOR

Scale

0 10 20 30 40

ft

P. Bellis 199

	LANDING SHIP, TANK (Class 1)	LANDING SHIP, TANK (Class 2)
Operational use	British designed, ocean-going tank carrying ship capable of landing medium tanks over a bow ramp (and extension) directly onto beaches steeper than 1/37	US designed to land waterproofed tanks or vehicles over ramp on 1/50 beach slope
Description:	Designated 'Boxer Class', three ships, Boxer, Bruiser, Thruster. Troops and crew on first deck, vehicles on second. Stack off-centre to allow continuous tank deck, located midships with 40 ton crane.	US design, designated US LST-1 with a sub-class US LST-542 with slightly more displacement. Elevator & hatch service first deck from LST 513 onwards (less 531), otherwise serviced by ramp.
Capacity:	13x 40ton or 20x 25ton tanks plus 36x loaded 3ton lorries (150tons total) Troops 13 officers, 180 men	Ocean-going load 2100tons (LST-1) or 1900tons (LST-542). Troops 16 officers, 147 men or 14 officers, 131 men (2 or 6 davit ships)
Endurance:	8000 miles @ 14 kts (estimated)	6000 miles radius @ 9 kts
Speed:	17 knots (max)	10.8 knots (max)
Dimensions:	390ft 0in bp x 49ft 0in max beam	length 328ft 0in o.a. x 50ft 0in beam
Displacement:	loaded 5410tons, landing 3616tons	loaded 4080tons, landing 2160tons (LST-1 light 1490t, LST-542 light 1623t)
Draft:	5ft for'd, 13ft aft (landing)	3ft 1in for'd, 9ft 6in aft (landing)
Armament:	12x 20mm guns, 2x 4in mortars	1x 12pdr gun, 6x 20mm guns, 4x FAM
Armour:	not stated	15lb STS splinter protection
Crew:	25 officers, 137 men	7 officers, 204 men or 9 officers, 220 men (2 or 6 davit ships)
Fuel:	2100tons max	1060tons max
Propulsion:	T.S. Turbine 7000 h.p.	2x 900 h.p. diesels, twin screw

note: Landing Ship Tank (Class 3) ocean-going British adaptation of American LST design, incorporating steam propulsion. Built in the Far East.

	LANDING CRAFT, TANK (Mk 3)	LANDING CRAFT, TANK (Mk 4)
Description:	British design, longer than previous marks 1 & 2, lands tanks on beach slopes greater than 1/33. Can only be transported on Landing Ship Dock.	British design, developed from earlier marks to suit slope of Normandy Beaches, i.e. slopes greater than 1/150
Description:	Bow ramp, single cargo deck, bridge, stack and wheelhouse aft.	Bow ramp, single cargo deck, bridge, stack and wheelhouse aft.
Capacity:	5x 40ton tanks or 10x 3ton trucks or 300tons cargo.	6x 40ton tanks or 9x 30ton tanks or 12x loaded 3ton trucks or 350tons cargo.
Endurance:	1900 miles at 10½ knots 2700 miles at 9 knots	500 miles at 9½ knots 1100 miles at 8 knots
Speed:	10¾ knots max (loaded)	8 knots (max continuous) at 1375 r.p.m. 5 knots on single engine
Dimensions:	length 192ft 0in o.a., beam 31ft 0in	length 187ft 3in o.a., beam 38ft 8in
Displacement:	light, 350tons	light, 200tons
Draft: (light) (loaded tanks) (loaded trucks)	1ft 9in for'd, 5ft 3in aft 3ft 5in for'd, 6ft 8in aft 2ft 2in for'd, 6ft 0in aft	1ft 0in for'd, 3ft 10in aft 3ft 1in for'd, 4ft 3in aft 1ft 10in for'd, 4ft 0in aft
Armament:	2x 2pdr pom-poms or 2x 20mm guns aft of deckhouse	2x 20mm guns aft of deckhouse, Army 40mm can be fired en route as AA protection.
Armour:	15lb DIHT over wheelhouse, to conning tower and after reels; 15 or 20lb splinter protection to gun positions; 2½in plastic protection to compass platform. Armoured doors (gangways) in hold at bow	15lb plating to steering position, compass platform, gun positions, forward winches and 10lbs to anchor reels.
Crew:	2 officers, 10 men + vehicle crews	2 officers, 10men + vehicle crews
Propulsion:	2x Paxman 500 h.p. diesels, twin 40in screws and rudders	2x Paxman 500 h.p. diesels, twin 21in screws and rudders
Serial Numbers:	LCT 300 to LCT 499	LCT 500 to LCT 1364

LANDING CRAFT TANK MARK IV

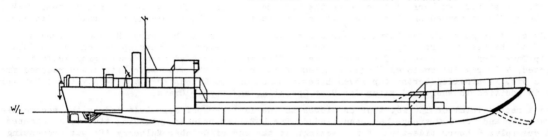

W/L

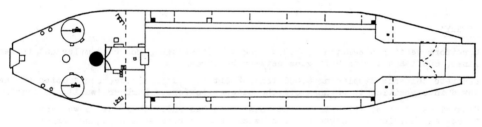

Scale

0   30   ft

P.W. Bellis

MULBERRY 'B' ARTIFICIAL HARBOUR

During the planning of the invasion, the need was recognised for the provision of artificial harbours to ensure sheltered water for berthing and operating ship-to-shore craft at both high and low tides. Two harbours were built, codenamed 'Mulberry', the simpler Mulberry 'A' to serve the U.S. Beaches and Mulberry 'B' at Arromanches. Work on construction of Mulberry 'B' commenced on 10th June 1944 and the East Stores Pier commenced operating 14th June.

From 19th to 22nd June, heavy gales in the Channel caused considerable damage to Mulberry 'B' and destroyed Mulberry 'A' apart from the breakwaters. Repairs were made and the Centre Pier commenced operation on 7th July and the Landing Ship Tank Pier on 17th July. The fourth (West) Pier was designated as a discharging jetty for barges. When completed, Mulberry 'B' enclosed 2 square miles of water where the mean wave height was reduced from approximately 8ft to 3ft. It provided berths for seven Liberty ships of 7,000 tons each and twenty-three Coasters of 2,000 tons each in addition to sheltered water for Port Operating and Repair Craft.

The Harbour handled a record total of 136,164 tons of stores in the last week of July 1944 and by the second week in August 10,000 vehicles and 120,000 troops had been landed. The LST Pier reduced unloading time to 23 minutes in comparison to 2½ hours (plus 6 hours tide-turn) for beaching. At the end of October Mulberry 'B' was processing 25% of the stores, 20% of the personnel and 15% of the vehicles for 21st Army Group. From the Invasion date to 19th November 1944, when the Port was finally closed, a total of 239,000 tons had been unloaded via pierheads and a further 290,000 tons direct from ship to shore via barges and DUKWs. Dismantling of the Port commenced December.

TERMS EMPLOYED ON 'MULBERRY'

BOMBARDONS:	Cruciform section steel tanks, 200ft long x 25ft section, moored 3 miles out to sea in two lines, 800ft apart with 50ft gaps between bombardons.
PHOENIXES:	Concrete caissons displacing 6,000 tons, 200ft long x 50ft wide, constructed in the UK and towed into position to be sunk off the beaches to form a harbour 'wall'. 31 constructed.
GOOSEBERRIES:	Unserviceable ships which travelled to Arromanches under their own power and were then sunk to act as individual blockships or crescent-shaped breakwaters (Gooseberries).
WHALES:	Pier head pontoons 200ft long x 60ft wide x 10ft deep displacing 1100 tons each. Fitted with four 'spud' legs, 80ft high x 4ft square and weighing 35 tons each, which moved vertically at 2½ft/min powered by their own 20hp winch. Six Whales were used.
INTERMEDIATE PONTOONS:	Used for joining 'whales', these were 80ft x 60ft wide sections, rigidly fixed to the whale at one end and to the adjacent whale via an incorporated telescopic span.

LST PIERHEAD: Formed from two 'whales' forming a 'T' shape and linked by a telescopic span, one aligned with the roadway, the other at rightangles. Incorporated gravity fenders on berthing sides and a ramp-type buffer which could be approached by the LST at 3 knots, reduced to stop.

FLOATING ROADWAY: Used to form a link between Pierhead and shore, formed from joined 80ft long sections with 10ft wide non-slip decking supported by cross-girders. Spherical bearings allowed up to 40 degrees of twist along the length of each span and a telescopic section was included at one end of the road length allowing adjustment between 80ft and 71ft. The 28 ton sections were supported on two episoidal floats each 42ft x 15ft x 8ft deep anchored to the sea bed by kite anchors. Floats weighed 16tons each.

PIPE LINE UNDER THE OCEAN (P.L.U.T.O.)

Two pipelines were laid under the Channel to allow bulk fuel to be supplied directly from the UK to the Armies in France.

First pipeline laid from Isle of Weight to Cherbourg (Bambi Near; Bambi Far) and operated from 18th September to 4th October 1944 pumping a total of almost 1,000,000 gallons.

The second pipeline from Dungeness, Kent to Boulogne (Dumbo Near; Dumbo Far) operated from 27th October 1944 to 31st August 1945 pumping an average 3,500 tons (1,000,000 gals) daily. Piped POL reached Rouen 8th September 1944. Advanced port for bulk petrol storage was Ostend, accepting first tanker discharge on 29th September 1944.

Construction and maintenance was the responsibility of the Royal Engineers, operation was carried out by RASC units (7 Bulk Storage Coy (UK) and 8 Bulk Storage Coy (Europe))

PORTS AVAILABLE TO 21st ARMY GROUP

Mulberry 'B'	from 10th June 1944 (see above)
Ostend	liberated 10th September 1944
Le Havre	liberated 12th September, extensive damage
Calais	liberated 30th September, heavy damage
Antwerp	liberated 4th September, estuary cleared 26th November for first convoy (28.11)

DAKOTA TRANSPORT WITH 'D-DAY' STRIPES

2nd TACTICAL AIR FORCE

GROUP	WING	SQUADRONS (mid 1944)	SQUADRONS (post Sept 1944)	AIRCRAFT
2	136		418(Cdn), 605	Mosquito VI
	137	226	226, 342(Fr)	Mitchell II
		88, 342(Fr)		Boston IIIA
	138	107, 613, 305(Pol)	107, 613, 305(Pol)	Mosquito VI
	139	98, 180, 320(Dutch)	98, 180, 320(Dutch)	Mitchell II
	140	21, 464(Aus), 487(NZ)	21, 464(Aus), 487(NZ)	Mosquito VI
83	39	400(Cdn)	400(Cdn), 414(Cdn), 430(Cdn)	Spitfire XI
		168, 414(Cdn), 430(Cdn)		Mustang I
	121	174, 175, 245	175, 184, 245	Typhoon IB
	122	19, 65, 122		Mustang III
			3, 56, 80, 486(NZ)	Tempest
			616	Meteor
	124	181, 182, 247	137, 181, 182, 247	Typhoon IB
	125	132, 453(Cdn), 602	41, 130, 350(Belg)	Spitfire IX
	126	401(Cdn), 411(Cdn), 412(Cdn)	401(Cdn), 402(Cdn), 411(Cdn), 412(Cdn)	Spitfire IX
	127	403(Cdn), 416(Cdn), 421(Cdn)	403(Cdn), 416(Cdn), 421(Cdn), 443(Cdn)	Spitfire IX
	129	184		Typhoon IB
	143	438(Cdn), 439(Cdn), 440(Cdn)	438(Cdn), 439(Cdn), 440(Cdn)	Typhoon IB
	144	441(Cdn), 442(Cdn), 443(Cdn)		Spitfire IX
84	35	2, 268	2, 4, 268	Mustang IA
		4		Spitfire IX
	123	198, 609	164, 183, 198, 609	Typhoon IB
	131	302(Pol), 308(Pol), 317(Pol)	302(Pol), 308(Pol), 317(Pol)	Spitfire IX
	132	66, 331(Nor), 332(Nor)	66, 127, 322(Dutch)	Spitfire IX
	133	129, 306(Pol), 315(Pol)		Mustang III
	134	310(Cz), 312(Cz), 313(Cz)		Spitfire IX
	135	222, 349(Belg), 485(NZ)	349(Belg)	Spitfire IX
			33, 222, 274	Typhoon IB
	136	164, 183		Typhoon IB
	145	329(Fr), 340(Fr), 341(Fr)	74, 340(Fr), 341(Fr), 345(Fr), 485(NZ)	Spitfire IX
	146	193, 197, 257, 266	193, 197, 257, 266	Typhoon IB

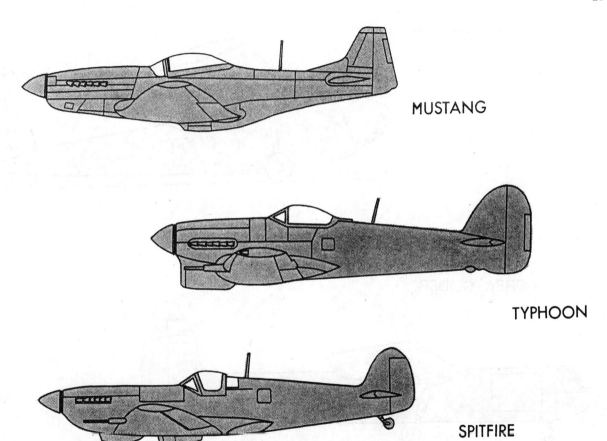

MUSTANG

TYPHOON

SPITFIRE

19

HAMILCAR GLIDER

HORSA GLIDER

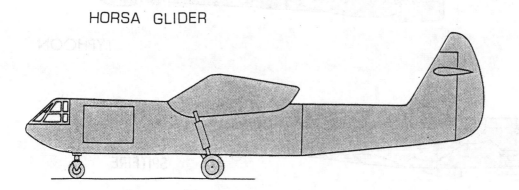

SECOND TACTICAL AIR FORCE

GROUP	WING	SQUADRONS (mid 1944)	SQUADRONS (post Sept 1944)	AIRCRAFT
--	34		16	Spitfire
			69	Wellington
			140	Mosquito
85	142		276 Air/Sea Rescue	Walrus-Spitfire
	148		264, 409(Cdn)	Mosquito
	149		219, 410(Cdn), 488(Cdn)	Mosquito
38		295, 296, 297, 570	295, 190, 196,299, 570, 620	Albemarle/Horsa
		190, 196, 299, 620	296, 297, 298, 644	Stirling IV/Horsa
		298, 644		Halifax/Horsa
			161 (Special Duties)	or Halifax/Hamilcar
				Stirling/Hudson
46		48, 233, 271, 512, 575	48, 233, 271, 437(Cdn), 512, 575	Dakota/Horsa

US 9th AIR FORCE (IX TROOP-CARRIER COMMAND)

52 Wing (61,313,314,315,316,349 Gps), 53 Wing (434,435,436,437,438 Gps), 50 Wing (439,440,441,442, Pathfinder Gps)

All equipped with Dakota C47, some C46 in March 1945. Note: RAF Wing= USAAF Group, RAF Group= USAAF Wing

TYPICAL AIRLIFT CAPABILITY

Airlanding Brigade : 490x Horsa, 24x Hamilcar & Tugs. Parachute Brigade : 126x Dakota, 27x Horsa, 3x Hamilcar
Dakota Lift: 25 paratroops or 3.9tonnes cargo, Horsa Lift: 29-32 Tps or jeep with towed gun (3.6tonnes cargo)
Hamilcar Lift: Cargo only, payload 7.9tonnes (able to carry light tank).

The C53 Skytrooper (Dakota II) was also employed and differed from the C47 Skytrain (Dakota I) by being solely used as a troop transport, differences including a small access door and fixed metal seats in the fuselage.

21

D.U.K.W. AMPHIBIOUS TRUCK

ORDER OF BATTLE

THE ASSAULT LANDINGS

6th-7th JUNE 1944

PEGASUS BRIDGE OVER THE ORNE CANAL, NORMANDY

6th AIRBORNE DIVISION - ASSAULT

DIVISIONAL TROOPS:

HQ 6th Airborne Division

Divisional Signals

22 Independent Parachute Coy

6 Airborne Divn Regt RAC (Recce)

53 Airlanding Light Regt RA (211 Bty)
3 Airlanding Anti-Tank Bty RA
4 Airlanding Anti-Tank Bty RA*

3 & 591 Parachute Sqns RE
249 Fld Coy (Airborne) RE* (less dets)

224 & 225 Para Field Ambulance RAMC
195 Airlanding Field Ambulance RAMC

6 Airborne Division Workshop REME

398 Composite Coy RASC*
716 Light Composite Coy RASC

UNDER COMMAND FOR ASSAULT PHASE

1 & 2 Wings Glider Pilot Regiment

36 L of C Transport Column RASC
233 Troop Carrier Coy RASC
749 & 799 Air Despatch Coys RASC

BRIGADES:

3rd PARACUTE BRIGADE

  8Bn Parachute Regt
  9Bn Parachute Regt
  1(Cdn)Bn Parachute Regt

5th PARACHUTE BRIGADE

  7Bn Parachute Regt
  12Bn Parachute Regt
  13Bn Parachute Regt

6th AIRLANDING BRIGADE

  2 Oxford & Bucks Light Inf (less det)
  1 Royal Ulster Rifles
  12 Devonshire Regt (less 'A' Coy)
  'A' Coy, 12 Devonshire Regt*

DETATCHED UNITS (Bridges at Benouville, Ranville)

  2 Oxford & Bucks Light Inf
  (two Plns 'B' Coy & 'D' Coy)

  249 Fld Coy (Airborne) RE - details

  * units landed by sea

50th (NORTHUMBRIAN) INFANTRY DIVISION - ASSAULT

DIVISIONAL TROOPS:

HQ 50th Infantry Division
50 Infantry Divn Signals
50 Infantry Divn Provost Coy

61st Reconnaissance Regt RAC

2 Cheshire Regiment (MG)

149, 186 & 200 Fld Ambulance RAMC
22 Field Hygiene Section

233, 295 & 505 Field Coys RE
235 Field Park Coy RE

90 Fld Regt (SP) RA (357, 358, 465 Btys)
102 Anti-Tank Regt RA (99 & 288 Btys)
25 LAA Regt RA (82 Bty)

BRIGADES:

69th INFANTRY BRIGADE

5 East Yorkshire Regiment
6 Green Howards
7 Green Howards

151st INFANTRY BRIGADE

6 Durham Light Infantry
8 Durham Light Infantry
9 Durham Light Infantry

231st INFANTRY BRIGADE

2 Devonshire Regiment
1 Hampshire Regiment
1 Dorset Regiment

UNDER COMMAND FOR ASSAULT PHASE:

Westminster Dragoons (Sherman Crab Flails)
141 Regt RAC - two Tps (Crocodile Flame-Throwers)

6 Assault Regt RE - HQ, 81 & 82 Sqns (AVRE)
73 & 280 Fld Coys RE

Royal Navy Beach Commando 'J', 'Q' & 'T'

47 RM Commando
1 RM Armd Support Regt (1 & 2 Btys) - Centaurs

203 Fld and 168 Light Fld Ambulance

86 Army Fld Regt (SP) RA (341, 342, 462 Btys)
147 Army Fld Regt (SP) RA (413, 431, 511 Btys)
73 Anti-Tank Regt RA (198, 234 Btys)
93 LAA Regt RA (320 Bty)
120 LAA Regt RA (HQ, 394, 395 Btys)
HQ 113 HAA Regt RA, 152 AA Ops Room
356 Searchlight Battery - one Tp
662 Air OP Sqn - ground crew - one Flight

104 BEACH SUB-AREA (9 & 10 BEACH GROUPS)

8th ARMOURED BRIGADE (Sherman DD Tanks)

4/7 Dragoon Guards
Nottinghamshire Yeomanry

56th INFANTRY BRIGADE

2 South Wales Borderers
2 Gloucestershire Regiment
2 Essex Regiment

3rd INFANTRY DIVISION - ASSAULT

DIVISIONAL TROOPS:

HQ 3rd Infantry Division
3 Infantry Divn Signals
3 Infantry Divn Provost Coy

3 Reconnaissance Regt RAC

2 Middlesex Regiment (MG)

8, 9 & 223 Fld Ambulance RAMC

17, 246 & 253 Field Coys RE
15 Field Park Coy RE

7 Fld Regt (SP) RA (9, 16, 17/43 Btys)
33 Fld Regt (SP) RA (101, 109, 113/114 Btys)
76 Fld Regt (SP) RA (302, 303, 354 Btys)
20 Anti-Tank Regt RA (41, 45, 67, 101 Btys)

BRIGADES:

  8th INFANTRY BRIGADE

      1 Suffolk Regiment
      2 East Yorks Regiment
      1 South Lancs Regiment

  9th INFANTRY BRIGADE

      2 Lincolnshire Regiment
      1 Kings Own Scottish Borderers
      2 Royal Ulster Rifles

  185th INFANTRY BRIGADE

      2 Warwickshire Regiment
      1 Royal Norfolk Regiment
      2 Kings Shropshire Light Infantry

UNDER COMMAND FOR ASSAULT PHASE

GHQ Liaison Regiment (Phantom) - five patrols

22 Dragoons RAC (Sherman Crab Flails)

5 Assault Regt RE - HQ, 77 & 79 Sqns (AVRE)
629 Fld Sqn, 71 & 263 Fld Coys RE

Royal Navy Beach Commando 'F' & 'R'

41 Royal Marine Commando

5 Indpdt Armd Support Bty (SP) RM - three Tps (Centaurs)

106 Bridging & 90 Armd Bde Coys RASC

HQ 53 Medium Regt RA
9 Survey Regiment RA (one bty)
73 LAA Regt RA (HQ & 218 Bty)
92 LAA Regt RA (318 Bty - one Tp)
93 LAA Regt RA (322 Bty)
652 Air OP Sqn - ground crew - 'B' Flight

101 BEACH SUB AREA (5 & 6 BEACH GROUPS)

27th ARMOURED BRIGADE (Sherman DD Tanks)

      13/18 Hussars
      Staffordshire Yeomanry
      East Riding Yeomanry

1st SPECIAL SERVICE BRIGADE

      3, 4 & 6 Commando
      10(IA) Commando - two Tps Fr Fusilier Marin
      45 RM Commando, RM Engr Cdo - one Tp

3rd CANADIAN INFANTRY DIVISION - ASSAULT

DIVISIONAL TROOPS:

HQ 3rd Cdn Infantry Division
3 Cdn Infantry Divn Signals

Cameron Highlanders of Ottowa (MG)

14, 22 & 23 Fld Ambulance RCAMC

6, 16 & 18 Field Coys RCE

12 Cdn Fld Regt (SP) RCA (14, 16, 43 Btys)
13 Cdn Fld Regt (SP) RCA (22, 44, 78 Btys)
14 Cdn Fld Regt (SP) RCA (34, 66, 81 Btys)
4 Cdn LAA Regt RCA (32 Bty)

BRIGADES:

7th CDN INFANTRY BRIGADE

Royal Winnipeg Rifles
Regina Rifle Regiment
1 Canadian Scottish

8th CDN INFANTRY BRIGADE

Queens Own Rifles of Canada
Regiment de la Chaudiere
North Shore (New Brunswick) Regt

9th CDN INFANTRY BRIGADE

Highland Light Infantry of Canada
Stormont, Dundas & Glengarry Highlanders
North Nova Scotia Highlanders

UNDER COMMAND FOR ASSAULT PHASE

Inns of Court Regiment RAC ('C' Sqn) - Armd Cars

26 & 80 Assault Sqns RE (AVRE)
262 Fld Coy RE, 5 Fld Coy RCE

30 Assault Unit RM (detail)
RM Engr Cdo Landing Craft Obstacle
     Clearance Units Nos 7-12

Royal Navy Beach Commando 'L', 'P' & 'S'

2 RM Armd Support Regt (HQ, 3 & 4 Btys) - Centaurs

19 Cdn Field Regt (SP) RCA (55, 63, 99 Btys)
62 Anti-Tank Regt RA (HQ, 245, 248 Btys)
73 LAA Regt RA (218, 220 Btys)
114 LAA Regt (HQ, 372, 375 Btys)
          (321 Bty (97 LAA Regt))
80 AA Bde Tac HQ, 155 & 160 AA Ops Rooms
474 Searchlight Bty - two Tps
652 Air OP Sqn - ground crew - 'A' Flight

102 BEACH SUB-AREA (7 & 8 BEACH GROUPS)

2nd CDN ARMOURED BRIGADE (Sherman DD Tanks)

6th Armoured Regt (1st Hussars)
10th Armoured Regt (Fort Garry Horse)
27th Armoured Regt (Sherbrooke Fusiliers)

4th SPECIAL SERVICE BRIGADE

48 RM Commando, RM Engr Commando - one section

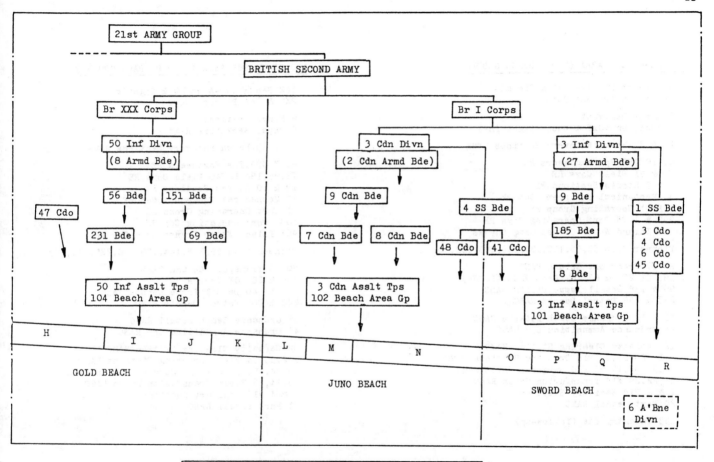

DIAGRAMATIC VIEW OF D-DAY ASSAULT - 6th JUNE 1944

101 BEACH SUB-AREA (5 & 6 BEACH GROUPS)

101 Beach Sub-Area HQ & Signals
241 & 245 Provost Coys

5 Kings Regiment
1 Bucks Bn (Oxf & Bucks Light Inf)

20 & 21 Beach Recovery Sections REME

HQ 18 GHQ Tps Engineers RE
84 & 91 Field Coys RE
8 & 9 Stores Sections RE
50 Mechanical Equipment Sec RE
9 Port Operating Group RE
999 & 1028 Port Operating Coys RE
940 Inland Water Transp Optg Coy RE

Pioneer Coys 53,85,102,129,149,267,292,303

HQ 21 Transport Column RASC
39,101,299 & 633 GT Coys RASC (DUKWs)
96 & 138 Detail Issue Depots RASC
237 & 238 Petrol Depots RASC

11 & 12 Ordnance Beach Details RAOC
44 Ordnance Ammunition Coy RAOC

16 Casualty Clearing Station RAMC
9,12,20,21,30 Fld Dressing Stations RAMC
37,38,39,40,55 Fld Surgical Units RAMC
21,22,29 Fld Transfusion Units RAMC
1 & 2 Fld Sanitary Sections
20 Port Detail RAMC

153 Infantry Bde (follow-up)

102 BEACH SUB-AREA (7 & 8 BEACH GROUPS)

102 Beach Sub-Area HQ & Signals
242 & 244 Provost Coys

8 Kings Regiment
5 Royal Berkshire Regt

22 & 23 Beach Recovery Sections REME

HQ 7 GHQ Tps Engineers RE
72,85,184 & 240 Field Coys RE
19 & 20 Stores Sections RE
59 Mechanical Equipment Sec RE
11 Port Operating Group RE
1034 Port Operating Coy RE
966 Inland Water Transp Optg Coy RE

Pioneer Coys 58,115,144,170,190,225,243,293

HQ 30 Transport Column RASC
199 & 282 GT Coys RASC
139 & 140 Detail Issue Depots RASC
240 & 242 Petrol Depots RASC

15 Ordnance Beach Detail RAOC
45 Ordnance Ammunition Coy RASC

32 Casualty Clearing Station RAMC
1,2,33,34 Field Dressing Stations RAMC
33,34,45,46,56 Field Surgical Units RAMC
13,14,36 Field Transfusion Units RAMC
3 & 4 Fld Sanitary Sections
21 Port Detail RAMC

104 BEACH SUB-AREA (9 & 10 BEACH GROUPS)

104 Beach Sub-Area HQ & Signals
240 & 243 Provost Coys

2 Herfordshire Regiment
6 Border Regiment

20 & 24 Beach Recovery Sections REME
XXX Corps Workshops REME (including
  two Composite Wksps & one Lt Recovery Sec)

69,89,90,183 Field Coys RE
21 & 23 Stores Sections RE
51 & 74 Mech Equipment Secs RE
1043 Port Operating Coy RE
953 & 961 Inland Water Transp Optg Coys RE

Pioneer Coys 75,173,209,280

305,536,605 GT Coys RASC
2 & 5 Detail Issue Depots RASC
244 Petrol Depot RASC

7,10,36 Ordnance Beach Details RAOC

3 & 10 Casualty Clearing Stations RAMC
3,25,31,32,35 Fld Dressing Stations RAMC
41,42,47,48 Fld Surgical Units RAMC
24 & 30 Field Transfusion Units RAMC
22 & 23 Port Details RAMC

RAF GROUND PERSONNEL

1304, 1305 Mobile Wing HQ RAF Regiment
104 & 107 Beach Sections
10582-3 Ground Controlled Interception Units
51 Beach Balloon Flight:
  Emergency Landing Strip Echelon
  Provost & Security Units
11 Air Formation Signals (½ Line Section)
16 Air Formation Signals (½ Wing Section)
21 & 24 Base Defence Sectors
Mobile Signals Units (83 & 85 Groups):
  543,554,582,585,5006,5030,5132,5141,
  5153,5160,5275

note:

ROYAL NAVY BEACH COMMANDO

11 Officers
 6 Petty Officers
67 Ratings

Signals Section (30 personnel)

SPECIAL AIR SERVICE REGIMENT

1 & 2 SAS Regiments
3 & 4 French Para Bns SAS
1 Belgian Bn SAS

AIR DESPATCH GROUPS RASC

WAR DEPARTMENT FLEET

GHQ LIAISON REGT (PHANTOM)

BEACH GROUPS

AIR FORMATION SIGNALS

AIRFIELD CONSTRUCTION GROUPS

ORDER OF BATTLE

GHQ, ARMY GROUP, ARMY & CORPS TROOPS

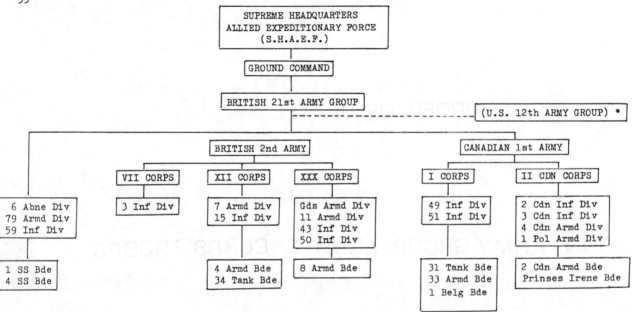

```
                    ┌─────────────────────────────────┐
                    │     SUPREME HEADQUARTERS         │
                    │ ALLIED EXPEDITIONARY FORCE       │
                    │      (S.H.A.E.F.)                │
                    └─────────────────────────────────┘
                                   │
                        ┌────────────────────┐
                        │   GROUND COMMAND    │
                        └────────────────────┘
                                   │
                    ┌──────────────────────────────┐               ┌──────────────────────────────┐
                    │  BRITISH 21st ARMY GROUP      │---------------│  (U.S. 12th ARMY GROUP) *    │
                    └──────────────────────────────┘               └──────────────────────────────┘
```

COMMAND STRUCTURE - 21st ARMY GROUP - 31st AUGUST 1944

* under command 1st August to 1st September 1944

UNITS IN HIGHER FORMATIONS

S.H.A.E.F.

Chief Engineer
Air Defence
Public Relations
Psychological Warfare
Signals Detatchment
European Allied Contact
HQ Command
Advocate General
HQ Section G1 - Personnel
HQ Section G2 - Intelligence
HQ Section G3 - Operations
HQ Section G4 - Supply
HQ Section G5 - Civil Affairs

SERVICES

3 GHQ Postal Unit
8 Base Post Office
5,8 Air Formation Postal Units
13,16,23 L of C Postal Units
2 GHQ Printing Press
6,12 Publications Depots
18 Stationery Depot
9,10 Mobile Duplicating Secs
4 Mot Transport Inspectorate

Pioneer Groups

6,8,10,11,13,14,15,16,20,21,22,
31,32,34,35,38,40,41,44,45,48,
49,50,56,58,60,62,63,78,79,86,
98,101,102,103

21st ARMY GROUP

Arm of Service Commands
Group Signals Detachment
Deputy Director of Supply
HQ Base Workshop REME
GHQ Liaison Regt (Phantom)
Civil Affairs Staff
Provost Marshall
3,25 Mil Prisons & POW
Fld Punishment Camps 5,6,7,8,23
4 Inspector of Mil Prisons
Base Censor
Field Press Censor
HQ Catering
GHQ Troops
Allied Liaison Contingency
Army Kinema
Photo Interpretation Unit
Salvage Section
Works Director
Dep Judge Advocate General
Education Section
Chaplain's Department
Welfare Section
Camp Commandant
Court Martial Centre
GHQ 2nd Echelon
HQ Air Despatch Group RASC
2 Field Remount Depot
5 Vetinary Hospital
6 Vet & Remount Conducting Ctr

2nd BRITISH ARMY

Arm of Service Commands
HQ Army Troops Engineers RE
Director of Surveys RE
Asst Dir Supplies & Transport
HQ Transport Increment RASC
HQ Troops & Defence Company
Civil Affairs Staff
HQ Vehicle Park RAOC
HQ Postal Unit
Claims & Hiring
Army Kinema

Field Salv Depots 1,2,3
Salv Colln Ctrs 11 - 19
Fld Salv Units 7,12,17,26,34,39,45,46

4 R.Northumberland Fus (MG)
1,2 Special Air Service Regts
3,4 French Parachute Bns
1,2 Wings Glider Pilot Regt

Fire Brigades (1st Class)
53,54,60,61,62,63,64,65,78,79

Fire-Fighting Companies
103,104,105,106,107,108,109,110,111,
112,113,114,115,116,117,118,119,120

Fire-Boat Companies 122,123

RM 1 & 2 Armoured Support Regts
RM 5 Indpdt Armd Support Bty

ROYAL ENGINEERS

HQ Army Groups RE 10,11,12,13,14
GHQ Troops Engrs 4,7,8,13,15,18,48,59
Army Troops Engrs 2,6,7
L of C Tps Engrs 4,5,6,7,8,9,10,11,14

Airfield Constn Gps 13,16,23,24,25
Rwy Constn & Maint Gps 2,3,5,6
Port Constrn & Repair Gps 1,2,4,5,6
Port Constn & Repair Coys 930,935

Inland Water Transp Gps 2,3,4
Movement Control Gps 17,18,20
Port Optg Gps 2,6,8,9,10,11
Railway Optg Group 3
Port Floating Equip Coys 969,870

Army Survey Depots 9,20
Field Survey Depots 3,4,5,25
Survey Sections 1,2,3,4,5,9(Air)
Map Repro Sections 13,14,15,16,19

Engineer Base Depots 5,6,7
Engineer Base Workshops 4,5
Railway Workshop Groups 1,3
Mob Rwy Wksps 4,6,7,8,9,10,11,12
Amb Train Maint Secs 1,2,3,4

Transp Stores Group 1
Transp Stores Port Sec 1,3,5
Engr Stores Port Sec 41,42,43,44,45
Mach Spare Parts Secs 10,11,12,14,16,17,18
Engr Local Purch Secs 2,3,4,5,6

10 Heavy Mobile Print Section
Mobile Laboratories 1,2,3
Royal Engineers Training School

CRE(Works) 3,4,5,19,22,100,101,102,106,153,154,155,159,
160,163,168,169,175,176
Works Sections
200,201,203,204,205,206,207,208,209,210,211,
212,213,214,215,216,217,218,219,220,221,222,
225,228,230,pool
Stores Sections
8,9,17,19,20,21,22,23,24,32,33,34,46,47
Mechanical Equipment Units
1,2,3,4,41,42,43,44,50,51
Mechanical Equipment Sections
1,6,9,16,21,22,23,24,25,27,28,53,54,55,56,
59,61,62,65,66,67,68,69,74,77

2 (Mech Equipment) Transportation Unit

Electrical and Mechanical Units
11,14,41,42,43,44,45,46,47,48,49,62,64,65,
66,69,70,72,74,75,76,77,78,81 plns
1,55 sections

Bridging Platoons 13,15,16,24,26
Boring Platoons 6,8

Bomb Disposal Units RE
5,19,23,24,25 Coys : 14,16,18 plns :
26,48,49,53,58,95,96,105,108,136,141,147,
161,223,224,225,226,255,256 sections

Dog Platoons 3,4

ROYAL ENGINEERS

Field and Field Park Coys (see also divisions)

8,9,11,14,16,24,55,65,66,69,70,71,72,73,74,75,
78,84,85,88,89,90,91,92

100,101,104,105,106,113,116,117,118,120,125,
129,131,136,145,151,152,155,157,158,162,164,
165,167,168,174,176,179,180,181,182,183,184,
186,188,197

206,209,210,211,224,227,232,234,240,249,257,
260,261,262,263,265,274,275,276,277,278,279,
280,282,285,286,289,294,295,296,297

503,508,515,519,521,545,546,547,548,549,550,
552,556,575,582,583,584,593

600,603,607,608,614,619,620,623,629,653,654,
659,661,662,663,665,666,669,670,672,674,677,
681,688,689,690,693,695,696

703,704,705,710,712,716,718,719,720,722,724,
732,736,758,759,760,761,762,763,796

802,804,806,808,810,811,853,855,856,858,860,
866,868,869,873,876,879,883

923,924,025,926,927,930,931,933,934,935,936,
937,940,951,952,953,954,955,956,961,962,963,
964,965,966,968,969,972,976,977,978,979,981,
982,983,986,987,995,996,998,999,

1013,1018,1022,1024,1025,1026,1028,1032,1033,
1034,1035,1036,1043,1044,1045,1046,1047,1048,
1049,1050,1051,1052,1053,1055,1056,1057

SIGNALS

CSO S.H.A.E.F.
CSO Staff 2 Tactical Air Force
21 Army Group HQ Signals
2 Army HQ Signals
CSO 24 Base Signals
2 & 12 L of C Signals
5 HQ L of C Signals ATS

Air Formn Signals 11,12,13,14,15,16,17,18
2 Air Support Signals

1 Special Wireless Group ('R' Force)
  1 & 3 Light Scout Car Coys
  Mobile Secs 4,5,7,8,10,13,14,15,17,19,21,53,
          54,101,102,104,108,109,110,111,
          116,118

Railway Telegraph Sigs 4,5,6
84 Telegraph Operating Coy

Beach Signals B10,B13

Line Sections 1,153,154

Special Cipher Sections 2,4,5

1 Independent Admin Coy

3 Field Force Signals

Multi-Channel Secs 1,2,3,5,11,12,51,53,54,55

Signals Equipment Sections 1,4

258 Corps Del Sqn Signals Troop

ROYAL ARTILLERY

HQ Anti-Aircraft Brigades
31,50,74,75,76,80,100,101,103,105,106,107,5RM

Heavy Anti-Aircraft Regiments
60,64,86,90,98,99,103,105,107,108,109,110,111,
112,113,115,116,118,121,132,137,139,146,155,
165,174,176,183,3RM

Light Anti-Aircraft Regiments
4,20,26,32,54,71,73,93,102,109,113,114,120,
123,124,125,126,127,133,139,149,150,4RM

Field Regiments
61,86,90,98,110,116,143,147,150,191

Anti-Tank Regiments 62,63,73,86,91

Medium Regiments 3,51,69

Survey Regiments 4,7,9,10

Heavy Regiments 32,56

Super Heavy Regiments 2,61

Searchlight Regiments 1,2,41,42,54

RA (Garrison) Regiments
43,46,49,58,61,65,67,68

RA (Infantry) Regiments
600,601,606,607,608,609,611,612,613,614,616,
617,619,623,625,630,631,637

Forward Obs Units 1 & 2 (A'bne), 3(Coast)

Fire Command Posts 13,14,15,16

3 Army Group RA

HQ & Sigs 3 AGRA
6 Fld Regt RA
13,59,67,72 Med Regts
59 Heavy Regiment
319 Arty Coy RASC

5 Army Group RA

HQ & Sigs 5 AGRA
4 RHA Regt
7,64,84,121 Med Regts
52 Heavy Regiment
Arty Coy RASC

9 Army Group RA

HQ & Sigs 9 AGRA
9,10,11,107,146 Med Regts
3 Super Heavy Regiment
738 Arty Coy RASC

HQ RA Sound Ranging Unit
1,3 Loc Warning Radar Tps
'X' Special AA Radar Bty
100 Army Radar Battery
1 Special Training Section
1 Identification Troop

Air Observation Posts (RA/RAF)
83 Group: 652,653,658,659,622 Sqns
84 Group: 660, 661 Sqns

4 Army Group RA

HQ & Sigs 4 AGRA
150 Fld Regt RA
53,65,68,79 Med Regts
51 Heavy Regiment
Arty Coy RASC

8 Army Group RA

HQ & Sigs 8 AGRA
25 Fld Regt RA
15,61,63,77 Med Regts
53 Heavy Regiment
116 Arty Coy RASC

17 & 59 Army Groups RA
Headquarters & Signals

ROYAL ARMY ORDNANCE CORPS

15 A.O.D. Headquarters

15 Transport Supply Depot
15 General Stores Company
15 Stores Transit Sub Depot
15 Forward Trailer Section
15 Technical Stores Company
15 Rear Supply Depot

16 A.O.D. Headquarters

16 Technical Stores Company
16 Rear Supply Depot
16 General Stores Company
16 Motor Transport Stores Coy
16 Forward Trailer Section
16 Transit Vehicle Park
16 Vehicle Group
16 Returned Vehicle Park

17 A.O.D. Headquarters

17 Forward Trailer Section
17 Motor Transport Stores Coy
17 Stores Transit Sub Depot
17 General Stores Company
17 Technical Stores Company
17 Rear Supply Depot

3 Fld Factory Ammn Repair

Base Ammunition Depots
1,2,3,12,15,17

Inspectorate Army Equipment
21,22,23

Ordnance Maintenance Coys
1,4

Independent Ammunition Coys
32,51,52

Forward Maint Ammn Sections
58,59,60,61

Forward Maint Stores Secs
58,59,60,61,62,63,64

Beach Detatchments
7,9,10,11,12,13,14,15,16

Port Detatchments
31,32,33,34,35,36,37,38,
39,40,41,42,43,44,45,46,
47,48,49,50,51,52,53

Port Ammn Detatchments
31,32,33,34,35,36,37,38,
39,40,41,42,43,44,45,46,
47,48,49,50,51,52,53

Mobile Ammn Repair Units
21,22,23,24,35

Ordnance Sub Parks (Armd)
Guards, 107, 111

Ordnance Sub Parks (Infantry)
103,115,143,149,150,
151,153,159

Vehicle Companys
14,15,16,17

Base Industrial Gas Units
1,2,3

Army Industrial Gas Units
31,32,33,34

Army Kinema Sections
Y,35,36,37,38,39,43,
44,45,46,47,51,52

Base Laundry Units
2,3,4,34,35

Mobile Laundry & Bath Units
35,101,102,103,104,105,
106,107,108,109,110,111,
301,302,303,304,305,306,
307,308,309,310,311

ROYAL ARMY SERVICE CORPS - TRANSPORT

Order of Battle June 1944

GHQ, Army and Corps Car Companies	8	Artillery Platoons	65
Army Troops Composite Coys	2	Artillery Sections	9
Army Transport Coys	4	Tank Transporter Coy - 2nd Army	3
Corps Troops Composite Coys	8	Tank Transporter Coy - GHQ	6
Corps Transport Coys	4	Tank Transporter Coy - 1st Cdn Army	1
Armd Divn Transport Coys	3	Bridge Companys	3
Infantry Divn Transport Coys	8	General Transport Coy - 3-ton*	18
Armd Divn Troops Coys (Assault)	1	General Transport Coy - 6-ton	18
Armd Brigade Coys (Assault)	2	General Transport Coy - 10-ton	6
Armd Divn Troops Coys	3	Motor Ambulance Coys	4
Armd/Tank Brigade Coys	4	Ambulance Car Coys	4
Armd Brigade Coys (Independent)	6	Bulk Petrol Transport Coys	8
Infantry/Armd Brigade Coys	27	Air Dropping Platoons	12
Infantry Divn Troops Coys	8	Military Oil Barge Coys	2
Infantry Brigade Coys (L of C)	3	Harbour Launch Companys	1
Airborne Divn Composite Coys (Light)	2	Fast Launch Coy (DUKW Support)	1
Airborne Division Composite Coys	4	Troop Carrying Companys	10
Artillery Coys, Headquarters	15	Tipper Companys	6

* initially included 11x DUKW Coys, reduced to 3x DUKW Coys by July 1944

Significant Changes - September 1944 onward

a) One Tank Transporter Coy converted to load carrying by welding airfield track to trailer base and sides. Capacity of each vehicle was 16½ tons supplies or 36 tons ammunition or 10 tons petrol, oil & Lubricants.

b) 30x 3ton lorries additional to establishment issued to 4x GT Coys, 12x 800gal tankers additional to establishment issued to 7x bulk petrol transport coys, 2x 10ton GT Coys allocated 5ton trailers,

c) During September 1944, 2x RE Bridging Equipment Coys and 16x 4-pln GT Coys were formed in the UK and moved to the Continent

d) 16x Army Transport Coys reorganised as 14x 4-pln 3-ton or 6-ton Coys

note: 13x Belgian and 4x Netherlands GT Coys commenced training Dec 1944, all active by April 1945

SUMMARY OF SUPPLIES AND TRANSPORT ORGANISATION RASC

DIVISION	Bulk Breaking Point and Supply Point	Supplies, petrol and ammunition held in transport vehicles and with each unit		DIVISIONAL TRANSPORT
FORWARD MAINTENANCE AREA (2 per Corps)	Holding two days rations, one day Maint Stocks, 200,000 gals petrol, 3,500 tons ammunition	2x Detail Issue Depots 1x Petrol Depot 2x Composite Platoons		CORPS TRANSPORT (800-1000 tons/day)
ARMY ROADHEAD	10-20,000 tons stores & 20,000 gals packed petrol	2x Base Supply Depots 5x Petrol Depots 4x Detail Issue Depots 4x Mobile Field Bakeries 3x Mobile Petrol Filling Stations		ARMY TRANSPORT (RMA to Army Roadhead)
REAR MAINTENANCE AREA	Trans-shipment Areas (DUKW to Road Vehicles) 2,000 tons per day Beach Maintenance Area (supplied by sea)	CRASC Petrol Installations 14x Petrol Depot 6x Mobile Petrol Filling Ctrs	CRASC Supplies 8x Base Supply Depot 8x Det Issue Depot 2x Field Bakeries 8x Mob Fld Bakeries 2x Fld Butcheries	L of C TRANSPORT operates in area to rear of roadhead BARGES, COASTERS and PIPELINES

ROYAL ARMY SERVICE CORPS - STORES

Base Supply Depots
32,41,52,55,56,57,58,59,61,62,63,64,65,
66,67,68,76,77,78,79,80,81,82,83

Petrol Filling Companys
1,3,5,9,11,13,15,16,17,19,20,22,23,26,
28,33,35,36,39,47,48,50,53,54,58,59,62,
63,67,75,76,79,89,90,93,94,96,101,104,
106,109,111,114,115,117,118,127,128,930
132,133,143,147,164,165,168,170,171,172,
173,174,182,199,212,213,215,218,222,224,
226,227,229,249,250,252,254,257,262,279,
282,283,284,287,288,290,297,299,300,301,
302,305,310,311,318,319,321,322,323,324,
346,361,364,365,372,373,377,378,379,380,
388,398,399,401,403,432,435,450,451,452,
458,459,460,463,483,486,501,502,503,504,
505,506,507,508,510,511,512,516,522,524,
525,526,527,528,529,530,531,532,533,535,
536,538,545,547,551,552,557,559,560,571,
624,625,626,633,635,645,648,649,701,702,
703,704,705,706,707,709,710,711,712,713,
714,715,716,718,719,721,722,723,724,725,
729,737,738,739,740,741,742,743,744,745,
753,754,755,756,777,783,784,787,789,791,
838,844,845,846,847,904,905,917,919,921,

Petrol Depots
5,18,21,103,107,109,131,132,133,134,135,
136,137,138,139,140,141,206,211,218,221,
227,230,231,237,238,240,241,242,243,244,
245,246,247,248,261,262,263,264,265,266,
267,268,269,270

Detail Issue Depots
1,2,3,4,5,6,13,14,15,19,26,29,49,50,54,67,
73,82,95,96,97,98,99,100,102,104,107,109,
111,115,116,117,118,119,120,121,122,130,
131,132,133,134,135,136,137,138,139,140,
142,143,146,147,148,149,150,151,153,154,
155,156,157,158,159,160,161,163,164,165,
166,167,168,169,186,187,188,189,190,192,201

Field Bakeries
30,35,42,43,46,48,68,89,91,93,98,99,102,103,
104,105,106,108,109,116,117,118,119,120,121

Field Butcheries
30,33,35,36,37,38,39,46,47,48,49,50,51,52

Petrol Filling Centres
22,23,24,25,26,27,28,30,31,32,33,34,35,36,37,
38,39,40,41,42,43,44,45,46,50,54,57,58,59

Bulk Petrol Storage Coys 8,9,10,11,12,13,14,17

Petrol Technical Stores Depots 1 & 2

6 Petrol Tin Factory Operating Company

Petrol Installations 3,4,5,7,8

Port Detatchments
36,37,38,39,40,41,42,43,44,45,46,47,48,49,
50,51,52,53

Supply Units 1 & 11   **2 Boat Stores Depot**

Base Provision Offices 17,18,19,27

103 Base Canteen Depot

ROYAL ELECTRICAL & MECHANICAL ENGINEERS

CME HQ Base Workshop
1 Base Armament & General Workshop
2 & 3 Army Troops Workshop
4 General Troops Workshop
863 Rear Maintenance Depot

1 Armd Fighting Vehicle Inspectorate
 2,3 AFV Inspectorate Service Units
2 Unit Maintenance Inspectorate 'B' Vehicles
4 Motor Transport Inspectorate

L of C Recovery Coys 866,867,868,869
Recovery Coys 1,2,3,4,5,6
43 Light Recovery Coy
Beach Recovery Sections 20,21,26

Heavy Recovery Sections
 831,832,833,834,835,836,837,838,
 840,841,875,876,877,881,882,897

Light Recovery Sections
 851,852,853,854,855,856,857,858,872,873

1 Mobile Tyre Repair Unit
1 Scales Branch
1 Technical Section

Radio Maintenance Detatchments 860,861,862
1 Telegraph Communication Experimental Detail
908 Location Warning Radar Workshop

L of C Troops Workshops
 6,7,8,9,10,11,12,13,897,898

Engineer Equipment Workshops
 1,2,3,4,5,6

1 Engineer Assault Troops Workshop
1 Tank Brigade Workshop
49 Armd Personnel Carrier Workshop
318 Armoured Brigade Workshop

Tank Troops Workshops
 4,6,8,27,30,31,33,34

Armoured Troops Workshops
 Guards,7,11,825,827,828,829

Infantry Troops Workshops
 3,15,43,49,50,51,53,59

231 Infantry Brigade Workshop

LAA/Searchlight Workshops
 1,2,3,4,5,6,344,356,474,557

LAA Workshops
 4,20,40,54,73,89,92,93,94,
 113,119,120,123,126,133

HAA Workshops
 60,86,98,99,103,105,108,109,112,
 113,115,116,118,146,165,174

MEDICAL

General Hospitals RAMC

   6, 8, 9, 20, 23, 25, 29, 30, 32, 39, 67, 74,
   75, 77, 79, 81, 84, 86, 88, 94, 96, 101, 105,
   106, 108, 109, 110, 111, 113, 115, 121

Queen Alexandras Royal Army Nursing Corps

Convalescent Depots 5, 12, 13, 14, 15

Casualty Clearing Stations (CCS):

   3, 10 (XXX Corps); 16, 32 (I Corps); 32 (2 Army),
   33, 34 (VIII Corps); 23, 24 (XII Corps)

Field Surgical Units (FSU):

   6, 13, 14, 15, 27, 33, 34, 37, 38, 39, 40,
   41, 42, 43, 44, 45, 46, 47, 48, 49, 50, 51,
   52, 53, 54, 55, 56

Mobile Field Surgical Units 4, 5, 6

6 Mobile Neurological Surgical Unit

3 Chest Surgical Team

1 Vascular Injuries Section

Base Medical Depot Stores 5, 11, 12, 13, 16
Adv Depot Med Stores 8, 9, 11, 12, 14, 15, 16, 17

Mobile Bacteriological Laboratories 3, 4, 7, 8

Field Dressing Stations (FDS)

   1, 2, 3, 4, 9, 12, 20, 21, 24, 25, 30, 31,
   32, 33, 34, 35, 49, 50, 62

Field Ambulance:

   11Lt, 14Lt, 16Lt, 21Lt, 22Lt, 23Lt,
   168, 162, 163,

Dental Units RADC *

   Central Dental Centre (Eindhoven)
   Eastman Dental Clinic (Brussels)

   5 & 6 Maxillo-Facial Units

   Field Dental Centres   125, 147
   Mobile Dental Units   134, 204, 205, 206,
                           207, 208, 209, 210,
                           211, 212, 214, 215,
                           517, 526

Field Hygiene Sections:

   6, 22, 27, 30, 31, 45, 61, 68, 73, 80, 84, 85

4 Mobile Field Hygiene Laboratory

Field Sanitary Sections 1, 2, 3, 5, 6

* dental units also on establishment of hospitals
  CCS, FDS and Field Ambulance

ROYAL ARMOURED CORPS

HQ & Signals 79th Armoured Division

2 Armoured Replacement Group
  2 Armoured Delivery Regiment
  2 Armoured Refitting Unit

Army Delivery Squadron 256

Corps Delivery Sqns 254, 257, 258, 259

Forward Delivery Squadrons:
  261, 262, 263, 264, 265, 266, 267, 268,
  269, 270, 271

21 RAC Training Regiment

1 Recovery Unit - Enemy Equipment

ARMOURED BRIGADES:

4th, 6th (Guards), 8th, 27th, 30th, 31st,
33rd, 34th, Czec, 1 Cdn, 2 Cdn

TANK BRIGADES:

1st, 6th (Guards), 31st, 34th,

1st Armoured Engineer Brigade

ROYAL AIR FORCE REGIMENT

Armoured Squadrons:
  2742, 2757, 2777, 2781, 2804, 2806

Light Anti-Aircraft Squadrons:
  2701, 2703, 2715, 2734, 2736, 2760, 2786,
  2773, 2791, 2794, 2800, 2809, 2812, 2817,
  2819, 2823, 2824, 2826, 2834, 2838, 2845,
  2872, 2873, 2874, 2875, 2876, 2880, 2881

Rifle Squadrons:
  2713, 2717, 2719, 2724, 2726, 2729, 2731,
  2738, 2740, 2741, 2749, 2750, 2765, 2768,
  2770, 2786, 2798, 2805, 2807, 2811, 2816,
  2827, 2829, 2831, 2843, 2844, 2848, 2853,
  2856, 2862, 2863, 2865, 2868, 2871, 2879,
  2883

ROYAL AIR FORCE GROUND UNITS

Airfield Construction Wings:
  5352, 5353, 5354, 5355, 5357

Airfield Construction Squadrons:
  5001, 5002, 5005, 5006, 5007, 5008, 5009,
  5012, 5013, 5014, 5017, 5022, 5023

Balloon Wing 159

Balloon Sqns: 965,967,974,976,991,992,997,980

Balloon Unit 'M'

CANADIAN UNITS - HIGHER FORMATIONS

HQ Army Troops Area 1st Cdn Army

HQ 1st Cdn Army Civil Affairs Staff

1 Cdn Interrogation HQ Section

HQ 1 Cdn Army Meteorology Group
    Cdn Met Secs 11,13,15,20,22

1 & 7 Cdn Auxilliary Services

1 Cdn Army Car Section

Cdn Provost Sections 2,11,13

2 Cdn Field History Section

Signals

1 HQ Army Troops Signals Section

1 Cdn L of C Signals

1 Cdn Army Cipher Pool Section

3 Cdn Army Signals Park

2 & 3 Cdn WI/SW Sections

HQ 1 Cdn Air Liaison Group
    Air Liaison Sections:
    420,430,442,443,444,410,450,452,457,
    460,461,462,463,464,465,466,467,468

RCE

HQ 1 & 2 Cdn Army Troops Engineers
1 Cdn Army HQ Engineer Pln
HQ 1 Cdn Army Group Engineers

1 Cdn Army Field Survey Depot
HQ 2,3,4 Cdn Survey Companys
1 Cdn Landmark Unit

1 Cdn Railway Operating Group

1 Cdn Road Construction Coy

1 Cdn CRE (Works)
    Cdn Works Sections 1,2,3
    HQ 1 Cdn Mech Equip Coy
        Cdn ME Sections 1,2,3,4

        Cdn Elect & Mech Sections 2,3,4

1 Cdn Mechanical Equipment Park Coy

1 Cdn Workshop and Park Coy

1 Cdn Engineer Stores Section
1 Machinery Spare Parts (Base) Sec

1 Cdn CW Laboratory

Field Park Coys 8,10,11
Field Coys 20,23,29,30,31,32,33,34

RCASC

HQ RCASC 1 Cdn Army Troops
HQ RCASC 4 Petrol Installation
HQ 1 Cdn Army Transport Column
HQ 2 Cdn General Transport Column
33,34 Cdn Corps Troops Composite Coys
35,36 Cdn Army Troops Composite Coys
45,63,64 Cdn Army Transport Coys
66,69 Cdn General Transport Coys
65 Cdn Tank Transporter Coy
85,86 Cdn Bridging Coys
1 Cdn Mobile Printing Section
1,2 Cdn Increment MT Inspn Branch
121,136 Detail Issue Depots
247,248 Petrol Depots
1 Cdn Mobile Petrol Laborotory

ARTILLERY

16,156 Cdn AA Operations Rooms
1 Cdn Calibration Troop
HQ 2 Cdn Army Group RCA
  19 Fld Regt RCA
  3,4,7 Med Regts RCA
  2 HAA Regt RCA
  191 Fld Regt RA
  1 Heavy Regt RA

RCEME

HQ RCEME 1 Cdn Army
1 Cdn Army Troops Workshop
1,2 Cdn Engr Equipment Workshops
2 Cdn HAA Workshop
HQ 2 Cdn Recovery Coy
  4Hy & 7Lt Recovery Secs

RCAMC

Cdn General Hospitals
  1,2,3,4,5,6,7,8,10,12,16,20,21

Fld Surgical Units 5,6,7,8,9,10,11
Fld Transfusion Units 4,5,6,7
Field Ambulance 10,11,15,18
Field Dressing Stations 6,12,21
Field Hygiene Sections 8,12,13,14
Casualty Clearing Stations 2,3,6
Dental Coys 4,9
2 Cdn Army Dental Stores
2 Cdn Army Advance Depot Dental Stores

RCAOC

2 Cdn Corps and Army Troops Sub-Park
1 Cdn Ordnance Maintenance Coy
1,2 Cdn Ammunition Repair Units
Mobile Laundry & Bath Units 2,4,6,8,9

ARMOURED

25 Cdn Armd Delivery Regt (The Elgin Regiment)

INFANTRY

1 Cdn Army Defence Bn (Royal Montreal Regt)

LINES OF COMMUNICATION

Infantry:

  5 Kings Regt, 8 Kings Regt, 6 Border Regt,
7 E.Yorks Regt, 2 Hertfordshire Regt,
1 Bucks Bn (Oxf & Bucks LI), 18 Durham LI,
1 R.Berkshire Regt (to 4.45)

115th Infantry Brigade
  4 Northants Regt, 5 R.Berkshire Regt,
3 Monmouthshire Regt

116th (RM) Infantry Brigade
  27, 28 & 30 RM Regiments (Infantry)

117th (RM) Infantry Brigade
  31, 32 & 33 RM Regiments (Infantry)

301st (RA) Infantry Brigade
  616, 617 & 619 RA Regts (Infantry)

305th (RA) Infantry Brigade
  622, 624 & 639 RA Regts (Infantry)

306th (RA) Infantry Brigade
  626, 628 & 636 RA Regts (Infantry)

307th (RA) Infantry Brigade
  623, 635 & 631 RA Regts (Infantry)

308th (RA) Infantry Brigade
  627, 629 RA Regts (Infantry)

Garrison Regiments RA
  43, 46, 49, 58, 61, 65, 67, 68 Regts

L of C Sub Areas

7 Base SA	Antwerp, Duffel, Turnhout
8 Base SA	Hamburg
4 L of C	Kladow Airfield, Babelsburg
5 L of C	Tilburg, St Michielsgestel
6 L of C	Ostend, Rotterdam, Amsterdam, De Haan
9 L of C	Oost Dunkerke, Ostend, Bruges, Knocke
15 L of C	
16 L of C	Ghent, Oostakker, Tournai, De Haan
17 L of C	Lille, St Omer
18 L of C	
19 L of C	Burgsteinfurt
20 L of C	Brussels, Louvain, Thildonk, Zeventem
21 L of C	Eindhoven, Sonnis, Hasseldt

CIVIL AFFAIRS STAFFS

7 Civil Affairs Group (Netherlands)- 36x CA Detatchments

CA Detatchments

  2/19,20,123,201,202,203,204,205,206,207,210,213,214,
219,220,222,224,225,229,312,320,325,611,612,614,625,
629,714

CA Base Ports Depots 1 & 7

CA Inland Depots 2,3,4,5,6,8,9,10 (to 1.45)

Mil Govt Inland Depots 2,4 & 8 (from 1.45)

WD AUSTERITY CLASS 2-8-0

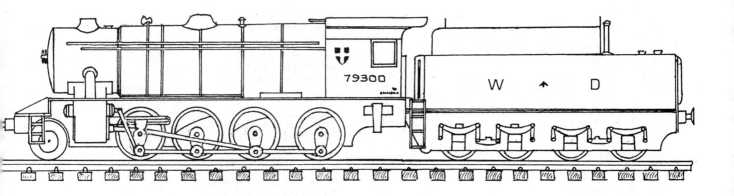

79300

W ↑ D

A total of 932 2-8-0s and 103 2-10-0s were shipped to the Continent between July 1944 and May 1945, all shipments until October 1944 being allocated to the U.S. Corps of Transport. Two vessels, 'Hampton Ferry' and 'Twickenham Ferry' were employed, both specially converted with 60-ton lifting gear at the stern. The British locomotives operated from sheds in France (Boulogne, Hazebrouck, Calais, Le Mans, Lille, Bethune, Dieppe, Acheres), Holland (Nijmegen, Roosendaal, Eindhoven, Tilburg) and Belgium (Antwerp, Mouscron, Aalst, Muysen, Ostend, Merelbeke, Hasselt, Schaerbeek, Tournai). In the first two months of 1945, eight Austerities were damaged or destroyed by enemy air attacks. Maintenance and repair was mostly carried out by Mechelen Royal Engineers Central Workshops in Belgium.

CORPS TROOPS (to November 1944)

HQ Corps & Corps Signals
Corps Defence Company
CBO and Staff

Corps Provost Company
Field Security (Mobile)
Corps Postal Unit
Pioneer Salvage Company
HQ Corps Reception Camp & Divnl Increments
Field Cash Office & Divnl Increments

Field Hygiene Section
Field Dressing Station
Casualty Clearing Station (x2)

HQ Corps Troops RA
   Anti-Tank Regiment
   Survey Regiment
   LAA Regiment
   Air OP Squadron

HQ Corps Troops RE
   Field Park Company
   Field Company (x3)

HQ Corps Troops Column RASC
   Corps Car Company
   Corps Troops Composite Coy (x2)
   Corps Transport Company
   Military Ambulance Convoy

HQ Corps Troops REME
   Corps Troops Workshop
   LAA Workshop

HQ Corps Troops RAOC
   Mobile Laundry & Bath Unit Type A
   Divnl Increment ML & BU Type B
   Ordnance Ammunition Coy/Sub Park

CORPS TROOPS (from November 1944)

HQ Corps & Corps Signals
Corps Defence Company

Corps Provost Co
Field Security (Mobile)
Corps Postal Unit
Pioneer Salvage Company
HQ Corps Reception Camp
Field Cash Office

Field Hygiene Section
Field Dressing Station

HQ Corps Troops RA
   Counter Bombardment Troops
   Air OP Squadron

HQ Corps Engineers Group
   Field Park Company
   Corps Engineer Regts (x2)
   Corps Field Park Coy

HQ Corps Troops Column RASC
   Corps HQ Carrier Company
   GT Company 3-ton
   GT Company 6-ton

HQ Corps Troops REME
   Corps Troops Workshop

HQ Corps Troops RAOC
   Corps Mobile Laundry & Bath Unit
   Ordnance Ammunition Coy/Sub-Park

CORPS TROOPS

I CORPS

HQ & Signals
I Corps Troops

62 Anti-Tank Regt RA
102 LAA Regt RA
9 Survey Regt RA
Air OP Squadron

Inns of Court Regt (Aug)

attached: 4 AGRA

VIII CORPS

HQ & Signals
VIII Corps Troops

91 Anti-Tank Regt RA
121 LAA Regt RA
10 Survey Regt RA
Air OP Squadron

2 Household Cav Regt (Aug)
Inns of Court Regt (Sept)

attached: 8 AGRA

XII CORPS

HQ & Signals
XII Corps Troops

86 Anti-Tank Regt RA
112 LAA Regt RA
7 Survey Regt RA
Air OP Squadron

Royal Dragoons

attached: 3 AGRA

XXX CORPS

HQ & Signals
XXX Corps Troops

73 Anti-Tank Regt RA
27 LAA Regt RA
4 Survey Regt RA
Air OP Squadron

11 Hussars (Aug)
2 Household Cav Regt (Sept)

attached: 5 AGRA

II CANADIAN CORPS

HQ & Signals
II Cdn Corps Troops

6 Anti-Tank Regt RCA
6 LAA Regt RCA
2 Survey Regt RCA
Air OP Squadron

18 Cdn Armd Car Regiment
   (12 Manitoba Dragoons)

attached: 2 Cdn AGRA

From November 1944, Anti-Tank, LAA & Survey Regts were withdrawn from Corps and re-allocated to Army command.

51

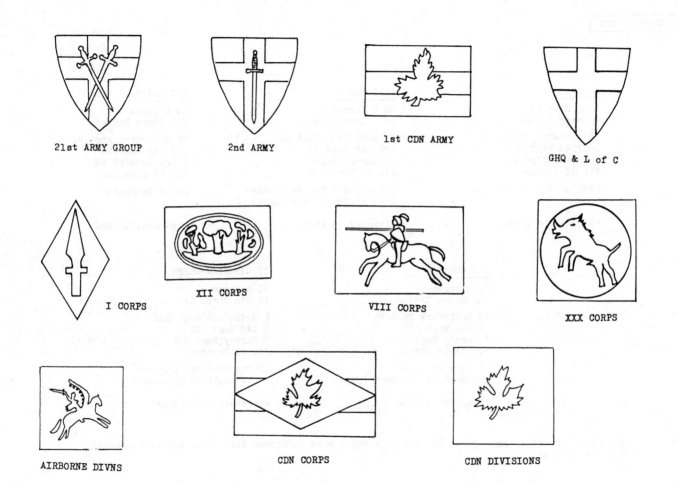

21st ARMY GROUP

2nd ARMY

1st CDN ARMY

GHQ & L of C

I CORPS

XII CORPS

VIII CORPS

XXX CORPS

AIRBORNE DIVNS

CDN CORPS

CDN DIVISIONS

GDS ARMD DIV   7 ARMD DIV   11 ARMD DIV   POL ARMD DIV   79 ARMD DIV

3 INF DIV   5 INF DIV   15 INF DIV   43 INF DIV   49 INF DIV

50 INF DIV   51 INF DIV   52 INF DIV   53 INF DIV   59 INF DIV

MOUNTAIN

53

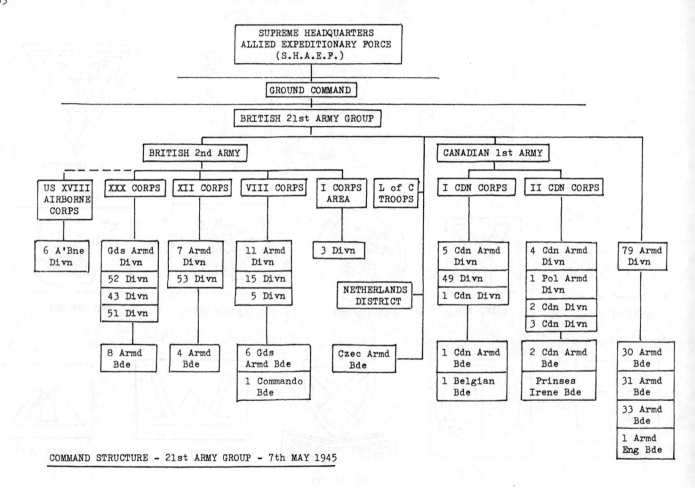

COMMAND STRUCTURE - 21st ARMY GROUP - 7th MAY 1945

ORDER OF BATTLE

DIVISIONS & BRIGADES

DIVISIONAL TROOPS NOT LISTED IN FOLLOWING ORDER OF BATTLE

ARMOURED DIVISION

HQ Employment Pln
Field Security Section
Postal Unit
Provost Company
Infantry Bde HQ Def Pln
Field Hygiene Section

Ordnance Field Park Coy

Divisional RASC
  Armoured Brigade Coy
  Infantry Brigade Coy
  Divisional Troops Coy
  Divisional Transport Coy

HQ Divisional REME
  Armoured Brigade Workshop
  Infantry Brigade Workshop
  LAA Regiment Workshop

  Light Aid Detatchments:
    Divn HQ (1), Armd Regts (3),
    Mot Bn (1), Armd Recce (1),
    Divn Sigs (1), RE Troops (1),
    Inf Bde (1), Fld Regt RA (2),
    Anti-Tank Regt RA (1)

AIRBORNE DIVISION

HQ Defence Pln
Field Security Section
Postal Unit
Provost Company
Para Bde HQ Def Pln (x2)
A'Lndg Bde HQ Def Pln
Forward Observer Unit
Mob Photo Enlargement Sec

Ordnance Field Park Coy

HQ Divisional RASC
  Airborne Light Coy
  Airborne Composite Coy (x3)

HQ Divisional REME
  Divisional Workshop

  Airborne Light Aid
  Detatchments (x7)

INFANTRY DIVISION

HQ Employment Pln
Field Security Section
Postal Unit
Provost Company
Infantry Bde HQ Def Pln (x3)
Field Hygiene Section

Ordnance Field Park Coy

Divisional RASC
  Infantry Brigade Coy (x3)
  Divisional Troops Coy

HQ Divisional REME
  Infantry Brigade Workshop (x3)
  LAA Regiment Workshop

  Light Aid Detatchments:
    Inf Bde (3), MG Bn (1),
    Recce Regt (1), Div Sigs (1),
    RE Troops (1), Fld Regt RA (3),
    Anti-Tank Regt RA (1)

note: above units may take title from units being served, e.g.
     159 Inf Bde Workshop REME, 11 Armd Division Troops Coy RASC
     This form is regularly used in place of individual unit no.

GUARDS ARMOURED DIVISION

HQ & Signals Gds Armd Divn
2 Welsh Guards (Armd Recce)
1 Independent MG Company

55 & 153 Field Regts RA
21 Anti-Tank Regiment RA
94 LAA Regiment RA

14 & 615 Field Sqns RE
148 Field Park Sqn RE
11 Bridging Troop RE

128 & 19Lt Field Ambulance
8 Field Dressing Station

5th GUARDS ARMOURED BRIGADE
  2 Armd Grenadier Guards
  1 Armd Coldstream Guards
  2 Armd Irish Guards
  1 Mot Grenadier Guards

32nd INFANTRY BRIGADE (GUARDS)
  5 Coldstream Guards
  1 Welsh Guards (to 3.45)
  3 Irish Guards (to 2.45)
  2 Scots Guards (2.45)

Division arrived ETO 28.6.44

7th ARMOURED DIVISION

HQ & Signals 7 Armd Divn
8 Hussars (Armd Recce)
3 Independent MG Company

3 & 5 Regiments RHA
65 Anti-Tank Regiment RA
15 LAA Regiment RA

4 & 621 Field Sqns RE
143 Field Park Sqn RE
7 Bridging Troop RE

131 & 2Lt Field Ambulance
29 Field Dressing Station

22nd ARMOURED BRIGADE
  5 Dragoon Guards (7.44)
  1 Royal Tank Regiment
  5 Royal Tank Regiment
  4 Cnty Lond Yeo (to 7.44)*
  1 Rifle Brigade (Motor)

131st INFANTRY BRIGADE
  1/5 Queens Regiment
  1/6 Queens Regiment (to 12.44)
  1/7 Queens Regiment (to 12.44)
  2 Devonshire Regiment (12.44)
  9 Durham Light Infantry (12.44)

Division arrived ETO 8.6.44

* merged with 3 Cnty Lond Yeo

11th ARMOURED DIVISION

HQ & Signals 11 Armd Divn
2 Northants Yeo (to 8.44)**
15/19 Hussars (8.44)
2 Independent MG Company

13 RHA & 151 Fld Regt RA
75 Anti-Tank Regiment RA
58 LAA Regiment RA

13 & 612 Field Sqns RE
147 Field Park Sqn RE
10 Bridging Troop RE

179 & 18Lt Field Ambulance
7 Field Dressing Station

29th ARMOURED BRIGADE
  3 Royal Tank Regiment
  23 Hussars
  2 Fife & Forfar Yeomanry
  8 Rifle Brigade (Motor)

159th INFANTRY BRIGADE
  4 Kings Shropshire L.I.
  3 Monmouthshire Regt (to 4.45)
  1 Herefordshire Regiment
  1 Cheshire Regiment (4.45)

Division Arrived ETO 13.6.44

** merged with 1 Northants Yeo

| 4th CANADIAN ARMOURED DIVISION | 5th CANADIAN ARMOURED DIVISION | POLISH ARMOURED DIVISION |

HQ & Signals 4 Cdn Armd Divn

29 Recce Regt (S.Alberta Regt)

5 & 23 Fld Regts RCA
5 Anti-tank Regt RCA
8 LAA Regt RCA

8 & 9 Fld Sqns RCE
6 Fld Park Sqn RCE

4th CANADIAN ARMOURED BRIGADE

21 Armoured Regt (Governor
   Generals Foot Guards)
22 Armoured Regt (Canadian
   Grenadier Guards)
28 Armoured Regt (British
   Colombia Regt)
Lake Superior Regt (Mot)

10th CANADIAN INFANTRY BRIGADE

Lincoln & Welland Regiment
Algonquin Regiment
A & S Highlanders of Canada

Divn arrived 31.7.44

HQ & Signals 5 Cdn Armd Divn

3 Armoured Regt (Governor
   Generals Horse Guards)

8 & 17 Fld Regts RCA
4 Anti-tank Regt RCA
5 LAA Regt RCA

5 Cdn Divn Tps Engrs

5th CANADIAN ARMOURED BRIGADE

2 Armoured Regt (Lord Strathconas
   Horse (Royal Canadians))
5 Armoured Regt (Princess Louises
   (New Brunswick) Hussars
9 Armoured Regt (British
   Colombia Dragoons)

11th CANADIAN INFANTRY BRIGADE

Perth Regiment
Cape Breton Highlanders
Irish Regiment of Canada

12th CANADIAN INFANTRY BRIGADE

Westminster Regiment
Lanark & Renfrew Scottish
4 Princess Louises Dragoon Guards

Divn arrived Feb/Mar 1945
(ex Italy)

HQ & Signals Polish Armd Divn

10 Polish Mounted Rifle Regt

1 & 2 Polish Field Regts
1 Polish Anti-tank Regt
1 Polish LAA Regt

Polish Armd Divn Tps Engrs

10th POLISH ARMOURED BRIGADE

1 Polish Armoured Regiment
2 Polish Armoured Regiment
24 Lancers   (Polish)
10 Dragoons - Mot (Polish)

3rd POLISH INFANTRY BRIGADE

1 Polish Highland Bn
8 Polish Infantry Bn
9 Polish Infantry Bn

Divn arrived 31.7.44

79th ARMOURED DIVISION

Reorganised in April 1943 to provide development of specialist armour and technique and advising on it's use. Elements of the division were allocated to line formations as required with Bde Command acting as advisor. The division came under direct command of 21st Army Group from May 1944, HQ arriving on Continent 12.8.44.

1st ASSAULT BRIGADE RE (6.8.44)

5 Assault Regt RE
  (26,77,79 Asslt Sqns)
6 Assault Regt RE
  (81,82,87 Asslt Sqns)
42 Assault Regt RE
  (16,617,222 Asslt Sqns)
149 Assault Park Sqn RE
557 Assault Training Est (1.45)
87 Assault Dozer Sqn RE (3.45)

30th ARMOURED BRIGADE (22.6.44)

22 Dragoons
1 Lothian & Border Horse
Westminster Dragoons

(Sherman Crab Flails)

addnl units:
  141 RAC Regt (7.44-9.44)
  11 Royal Tank Regt (12.44-1.45)
  4 Royal Tank Regt (3.45-4.45)

33rd ARMOURED BRIGADE (18.1.45)*

1 E.Riding Yeomanry
1 Northants Yeomanry
144 RAC/4 Royal Tank Regt

(Buffalo amphibians)

addnl units:
  11 Royal Tank Regt (Buffalo)

1st TANK BRIGADE (10.8.44)

11 Royal Tank Regt
42 Royal Tank Regt
49 Royal Tank Regt

(Canal Defence Lights)

(Bde dismembered for
  reinforcements, Bde
  HQ S/A 18.11.44)

31st TANK BRIGADE (9.44-2.45)*

141 RAC Regt (9.44)
1 Fife & Forfar Yeo (11.44)
11 Royal Tank Regt (11.44-12.44)
49 APC Regiment (12.44)
1 Cdn APC Regt (12.44)

(redes. 31 Armd Bde from
  2.2.45)

31st ARMOURED BRIGADE

141 RAC Regt
1 Fife & Forfar Yeo
7 Royal Tank Regiment

(Churchill Crocodile)

49 APC Regiment
1 Cdn APC Regiment

dates thus * indicate brigade already on Continent joins 79 AD, otherwise date arrived Continent.

These dates apply to brigade HQ, in some cases elements having arrived with D-Day Assault Force

| 1st AIRBORNE DIVISION | 6th AIRBORNE DIVISION | 3rd INFANTRY DIVISION |

1st AIRBORNE DIVISION

HQ & Signals 1 A'Bne Divn
1 Airlanding Recce Sqn RAC
21 Indpdt Para Coy AAC

1 Airlanding Light Regt RA
1 & 2 Airlanding ATk Btys
1 Airlanding LAA Bty RA

1 & 4 Para Sqns RE
9 Field Squadron RE
261 Field Park Sqn RE

181 Airlanding Fld Ambulance
16 & 133 Para Field Ambulance

1st AIRLANDING BRIGADE
  1 Border Regiment
  2 S.Staffordshire Regiment
  7 K.O. Scots Borderers

1st PARACHUTE BRIGADE
  1 Parachute Regiment
  2 Parachute Regiment
  3 Parachute Regiment

4th PARACHUTE BRIGADE
  10 Parachute Regiment
  11 Parachute Regiment
  156 Parachute Regiment

Division in ETO 17-27.9.44
in the Battle for Arnhem

6th AIRBORNE DIVISION

HQ & Signals 6 A'Bne Divn
6 Airborne Armd Recce Regt
22 Indpdt Para Coy AAC

53 Light Regiment RA
3,4 Airlanding ATk Btys (to 2.45)
2 Airlanding ATk Regt (2.45)

3 & 591 Para Sqns RE
249 Airborne Fld Coy RE
286 Airborne Fld Park Coy RE

195 Airlanding Fld Ambulance
224, 225 Para Fld Ambulance

6th AIRLANDING BRIGADE
  12 Devonshire Regiment
  2 Oxford & Bucks Light Inf
  1 Royal Ulster Rifles

3rd PARACHUTE BRIGADE
  8 Parachute Regiment
  9 Parachute Regiment
  1 Cdn Parachute Bn

5th PARACHUTE BRIGADE
  7 Parachute Regiment
  12 Parachute Regiment
  13 Parachute Regiment

Division in ETO (6.44-9.44),
(12.44-2.45), (3.45-5.45)

3rd INFANTRY DIVISION

HQ & Signals 3 Inf Divn
3 Recce Regiment RAC
2 Middlesex Regiment (MG)

7,33 & 76 Fld Regts RA
20 Anti-Tank Regiment RA
92 LAA Regiment RA

17,246 & 253 Fld Coys RE
15 Field Park Coy RE
2 Bridging Pln RE

8,9 & 223 Fld Ambulance
10,11 Fld Dressing Stns

8th INFANTRY BRIGADE
  1 Suffolk Regiment
  2 E.Yorkshire Regiment
  1 S.Lancashire Regiment

9th INFANTRY BRIGADE
  2 Lincolnshire Regiment
  1 K.O. Scots Borderers
  2 Royal Ulster Rifles

185th INFANTRY BRIGADE
  2 Warwickshire Regiment
  1 Norfolk Regiment
  2 Kings Shropshire L.I.

Division Arrived in ETO 6.6.44

5th INFANTRY DIVISION	15th (SCOTTISH) DIVISION	43rd (WESSEX) DIVISION

5th INFANTRY DIVISION

HQ & Signals 5 Inf Divn
5 Recce Regiment RAC
7 Cheshire Regiment (MG)

91,92 & 156 Fld Regts RA
52 Anti-Tank Regiment RA
18 LAA Regiment RA

245 & 252 Fld Coys RE
254 Fld Park Coy RE
18 Bridging Pln RE

141, 164 Fld Ambulance

13th INFANTRY BRIGADE
  2 Cameronians
  2 Wiltshire Regiment
  5 Essex Regiment

15th INFANTRY BRIGADE
  1 Green Howards
  1 K.O. Yorkshire Light Inf
  1 York & Lancaster Regiment

17th INFANTRY BRIGADE
  2 Royal Scots Fusiliers
  2 Northamptonshire Regt
  6 Seaforth Highlanders

Division arrived ETO 2.3.45
from CMF, Italy

15th (SCOTTISH) DIVISION

HQ & Signals 15 Inf Divn
15 Recce Regiment RAC
1 Middlesex Regiment (MG)

131,181 & 190 Fld Regts RA
97 Anti-Tank Regt RA (to 12.44)
102 Anti-Tank Regt RA (12.44)
119 LAA Regiment RA

20,278 & 279 Fld Coys RE
624 Fld Park Coy RE
26 Bridging Pln RE

153,193 & 194 Fld Ambulance
22,23 Fld Dressing Stns

44th INFANTRY BRIGADE
  8 Royal Scots Regiment
  6 K.O. Scots Borderers
  6 R.Scots Fusiliers

46th INFANTRY BRIGADE
  2 Glasgow Highlanders
  7 Seaforth Highlanders
  9 Cameronians

227th INFANTRY BRIGADE
  10 Highland Light Infantry
  2 A & S Highlanders
  2 Gordon Highlanders

Division arrived ETO 14.6.44

43rd (WESSEX) DIVISION

HQ & Signals 43 Inf Divn
43 Recce Regiment RAC
8 Middlesex Regiment (MG)

92,112 & 179 Fld Regts RA
59 Anti-Tank Regiment RA
110 LAA Regiment RA

204,260 & 553 Fld Coys RE
207 Fld Park Coy RE
13 Bridging Pln RE

129,130 & 213 Fld Ambulance
14,15 Fld Dressing Stns

129th INFANTRY BRIGADE
  4 Somerset Light Infantry
  4 Wiltshire Regiment
  5 Wiltshire Regiment

130th INFANTRY BRIGADE
  7 Hampshire Regiment
  4 Dorset Regiment
  5 Dorset Regiment

214th INFANTRY BRIGADE
  5 Duke of Cornwalls L.I.
  7 Somerset Light Infantry
  1 Worcestershire Regiment

Division arrived ETO 24.6.44

49th (WEST RIDING) DIVISION

HQ & Signals 49 Inf Divn
49 Recce Regiment RAC
2 Kensington Regiment (MG)

69 & 143 Fld Regts RA
185 Fld RA (to 11.44), 74 Fld RA
55 Anti-Tank Regiment RA
89 LAA Regiment RA

294,756 & 757 Fld Coys RE
289 Fld Park Coy RE
23 Bridging Pln RE

146,160 & 187 Fld Ambulance
16,17 Fld Dressing Stns

70th INFANTRY BRIGADE (to 8.44)
  10 Durham Light Infantry
  11 Durham Light Infantry
  1 Tyneside Scottish

146th INFANTRY BRIGADE
  4 Lincolnshire Regiment
  1/4 K.O. Yorkshire Light Inf
  Hallamshire Bn

147th INFANTRY BRIGADE
  6 Duke of Wellingtons (to 7.44)
  7 Duke of Wellingtons
  11 R. Scots Fusiliers
  1 Leicestershire Regt (7.44)

56th INFANTRY BRIGADE (8.44)
  2 S.Wales Borderers (to 4.45)
  2 Gloucestershire Regiment
  2 Essex Regiment
  7 R.Welsh Fusiliers (4.45)

Division arrived ETO 12.6.44

50th (NORTHUMBRIAN) DIVISION

HQ & Signals 50 Inf Divn
61 Recce Regiment RAC *
2 Cheshire Regiment (MG)

74,90 & 124 Fld Regts RA *
102 Anti-Tank Regiment RA *
25 LAA Regiment RA *

233,295 & 505 Fld Coys RE *
235 Fld Park Coy RE *
15 Bridging Pln RE

149,186 & 200 Fld Ambulance
47,48 Fld Dressing Stns

69th INFANTRY BRIGADE
  5 E.Yorkshire Regiment
  6 Green Howards
  7 Green Howards

151st INFANTRY BRIGADE
  6 Durham Light Infantry
  8 Durham Light Infantry
  9 Durham Light Inf (to 11.44)
  1/7 Queens Regiment (12.44)

231st INFANTRY BRIGADE
  2 Devonshire Regt (to 11.44)
  1 Dorset Regiment
  1 Hampshire Regiment
  1/6 Queens Regiment (12.44)

Division arrived ETO 6.6.44,
returned to UK as Training
division 12.44 less units *

51st (HIGHLAND) DIVISION

HQ & Signals 50 Inf Divn
2 Derbyshire Yeomanry RAC
1/7 Middlesex Regiment (MG)

126,127 & 128 Fld Regts RA
61 Anti-Tank Regiment RA
40 LAA Regiment RA

274,275 & 276 Fld Coys RE
239 Fld Park Coy RE
16 Bridging Pln RE

174,175 & 176 Fld Ambulance
5,6 Fld Dressing Stns

152nd INFANTRY BRIGADE
  2 Seaforth Highlanders
  5 Seaforth Highlanders
  5 Cameron Highlanders

153rd INFANTRY BRIGADE
  5 Black Watch
  1 Gordon Highlanders
  5/7 Gordon Highlanders

154th INFANTRY BRIGADE
  7 A & S Highlanders
  1 Black Watch
  7 Black Watch

Division arrived ETO 7.6.44

52nd (LOWLAND) DIVISION

HQ & Signals 52 Inf Div
52 Recce Regiment RAC
7 Manchester Regiment (MG)

70,80 & 186 Fld Regts RA
54 Anti-Tank Regt RA
108 LAA Regiment RA

202,241 & 554 Fld Coys RE
243 Fld Park Coy RE
17 Bridging Pln RE

157 Fld Ambulance

1 Mtn Regt RA (attached to 3.45)

155th INFANTRY BRIGADE
  7/9 Royal Scots Regiment
  4 KO Scottish Borderers
  5 KO Scottish Borderers (to 2.45)
  6 Highland Light Infantry (2.45)

156th INFANTRY BRIGADE
  4/5 Royal Scots Fusiliers
  6 Cameronians
  7 Cameronians (to 3.45)
  1 Glasgow Highlanders (3.45)

157th INFANTRY BRIGADE
  5 Highland Light Infantry
  6 Highland Light Inf (to 2.45)
  1 Glasgow Highlanders (to 3.45)
  5 KO Scots Borderers (2.45)
  7 Cameronians (3.45)

Division arrived ETO 15.10.44

53rd (WELSH) DIVISION

HQ & Signals 53 Inf Div
53 Recce Regiment RAC
1 Manchester Regiment (MG)

81,83 & 133 Fld Regts RA
71 Anti-Tank Regt RA
116 LAA Regt RA (to 12.44)
25 LAA Regt RA (12.44)

244,282 & 555 Fld Coys RE
285 Fld Park Coy RE
22 Bridging Pln RE

147,202 & 212 Fld Ambulance
13,26 Fld Dressing Stns

71st INFANTRY BRIGADE
  1 E.Lancs Regt (to 8.44)
  1 Highland Light Infantry
  1 Oxford & Bucks Light Inf
  4 R.Welsh Fusiliers (8.44)

158th INFANTRY BRIGADE
  4 R. Welsh Fusiliers (to 8.44)
  6 R. Welsh Fusiliers (to 8.44)
  7 R. Welsh Fusiliers (to 4.45)
  1 E.Lancashire Regt (8.44)
  1/5 Welch Regiment (8.44)
  2 S.Wales Borderers (4.45)

160th INFANTRY BRIGADE
  4 Welch Regiment
  1/5 Welch Regiment (to 8.44)
  2 Monmouthshire Regt
  6 R. Welsh Fusiliers (8.44)

Division arrived ETO 27.6.44

59th (STAFFORDSHIRE) DIVISION

HQ & Signals 59 Inf Div
59 Recce Regiment RAC
7 R.Northumberland Fus (MG)

61,110 & 115 Fld Regts RA
68 Anti-Tank Regt RA
68 LAA Regiment RA

257,509 & 510 Fld Coys RE
511 Fld Park Coy RE
24 Bridging Pln RE

203,210 & 211 Fld Ambulance
27,28 Fld Dressing Stns

176th INFANTRY BRIGADE
  7 S.Staffordshire Regt
  6 N.Staffordshire Regt
  7 Norfolk Regiment

177th INFANTRY BRIGADE
  5 S.Staffordshire Regt
  1/6 S.Staffordshire Regt
  2/6 S.Staffordshire Regt

197th INFANTRY BRIGADE
  2/5 Lancashire Fusiliers
  5 E.Lancashire Regt
  1/7 Warwickshire Regt

Division arrived ETO 27.6.44,
broken up 8.44, S/A 19.10.44

63

1st CANADIAN INFANTRY DIVISION	2nd CANADIAN INFANTRY DIVISION	3rd CANADIAN INFANTRY DIVISION
HQ & Signals 1 Cdn Divn	HQ & Signals 2 Cdn Divn	HQ & Signals 3 Cdn Divn
1 Royal Cdn Dragoons (Recce)	8 Cdn Recce Regt (14 Cdn Hussars)	7 Cdn Recce Regt (17 Duke of Yorks Royal Cdn Hussars)
Saskatoon Light Infantry (MG)	Toronto Scottish Regiment (MG)	Cameron Highlanders of Ottowa (MG
1 RCHA Regt, 2 & 3 Fld Regts RCA	4,5 & 6 Fld Regts RCA	12,13 & 14 Fld Regts RCA
1 Anti-Tank Regiment RCA	2 Anti-Tank Regiment RCA	3 Anti-Tank Regiment RCA
2 LAA Regiment RCA	3 LAA Regiment RCA	4 LAA Regiment RCA
1 Cdn Division Tps Engineers	2,7,11 Fld Coys, 1 Fld Pk Coy RCE	6,16,18 Fld Coys, Fld Pk Coy RCE

1st CANADIAN INFANTRY BRIGADE
Royal Canadian Regiment
Hastings & Prince Edward Regt
48th Highlanders of Canada

2nd CANADIAN INFANTRY BRIGADE
Princess Patricias Cdn LI
Seaforth Highlanders of Canada
Loyal Edmonton Regiment

3rd CANADIAN INFANTRY BRIGADE
Royal 22e Regiment
Carleton and York Regiment
West Nova Scotia Regiment

Divn arrived Feb/Mar 1945
from Italy

4th CANADIAN INFANTRY BRIGADE
Royal Regiment of Canada
Royal Hamilton Light Inf
Essex Scottish Regiment

5th CANADIAN INFANTRY BRIGADE
Black Watch of Canada
Le Regt de Maisonneuve
Calgary Highlanders

6th CANADIAN INFANTRY BRIGADE
Les Fusiliers Mont-Royal
South Saskatchewan Regiment
QO Cameron Highlanders
of Canada

Divn arrived 7.7.44

7th CANADIAN INFANTRY BRIGADE
Royal Winnipeg Rifles
Regina Rifle Regiment
1 Canadian Scottish

8th CANADIAN INFANTRY BRIGADE
Queens Own Rifles of Canada
Le Regt de la Chaudiere
N.Shore (New Brunswick) Regt

9th CANADIAN INFANTRY BRIGADE
Highland LI of Canada
N.Nova Scotia Highlanders
Stormont, Dundas &
Glengarry Highlanders

Divn arrived 6.6.44

INDEPENDENT BRIGADES

56th INFANTRY BRIGADE

2 S.Wales Borderers
2 Gloucestershire Regt
2 Essex Regt

(to 49 Divn 8.44)

1st SPECIAL SERVICE BDE

3 Commando
4 Commando
6 Commando
45 (RM) Commando

4th SPECIAL SERVICE BDE

41 (RM) Commando
46 (RM) Commando
47 (RM) Commando
48 (RM) Commando (IA)

1 POLISH PARA BDE

1 Polish Para Bn
2 Polish Para Bn
3 Polish Para Bn

CZEC ARMOURED BRIGADE

1 Czec Armoured Regt
2 Czec Armoured Regt
3 Czec Armoured Regt
Czec Motor Battalion
Czec Fld Arty Battery

4th ARMOURED BRIGADE

Royal Scots Greys
44 Royal Tank Regiment
3 Cnty London Yeo
2 KRRC (Motor)

8th ARMOURED BRIGADE

4/7 Dragoon Guards
13/18 Hussars (7.44)
24 Lancers (disb 7.44)
Notts Yeomanry
12 KRRC (Motor)

27th ARMOURED BDE

13/18 Hussars
Staffs Yeomanry
East Riding Yeo

(Bde disb 7.44)

6th GUARDS TANK BRIGADE

4 Tk Bn Grenadier Gds
4 Tk Bn Coldstream Gds
3 Tk Bn Scots Guards
4 Mot Coldstream Gds (2.45)

(redes 6 Gds Armd Bde 2.45)

31st TANK BRIGADE

7 Royal Tank Regt
9 Royal Tank Regt

(to 79 ADivn 9.44)

33rd ARMOURED BRIGADE

144 RAC Regt
148 RAC Regt (to 8.44)
1 Northants Yeomanry
E.Riding Yeomanry (8.44)
11 Royal Tank Regt (1.45)
(to 79 ADivn 1.45)

34th TANK BRIGADE

107 RAC Regt
147 RAC Regt
153 RAC Regt (to 8.44)
9 R. Tank Regt (9.44)

(redes 34 Armd Bde 2.45)

2nd CDN ARMOURED BDE

6 Armd Regt (1 Hussars)
10 Armd Regt (Fort Garry Horse)
27 Armd Regt (Sherbrooke Fusiliers)

1st CDN ARMOURED BDE

11 Armd Regt (Ontario Regiment)
12 Armd Regt (Three Rivers Regiment)
14 Armd Regt (Calgary Regiment)

1st BELGIAN BRIGADE

1,2 & 3 Mot Battalions
Belgian Armd Car Sqn
Field Arty Battery
Belgian Engineers

PRINSES IRENE BDE

1,2 & 3 Inf Battalions
Reconnaissance Sqn
Fld Arty Battery

GUARDS TANK BRIGADE

PRINSES IRENE BRIGADE

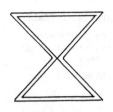

33rd ARMOURED BRIGADE

4th ARMOURED BRIGADE

22nd ARMOURED BRIGADE

27th ARMOURED BRIGADE

8th ARMOURED BRIGADE

1st BELGIAN BRIGADE

1st TANK BRIGADE and
31st TANK BRIGADE

34th TANK BRIGADE

2nd CANADIAN ARMOURED
BRIGADE

CZEC ARMOURED BRIGADE

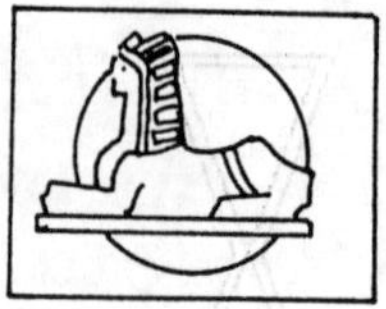

56th INFANTRY BRIGADE

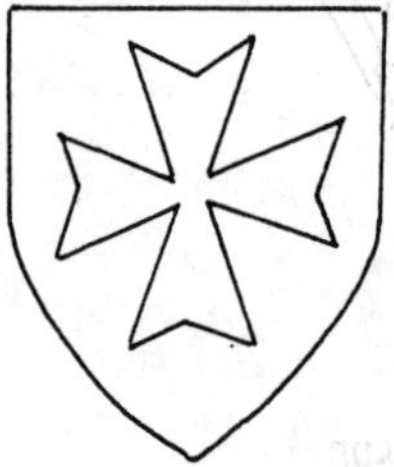

231st INFANTRY BRIGADE

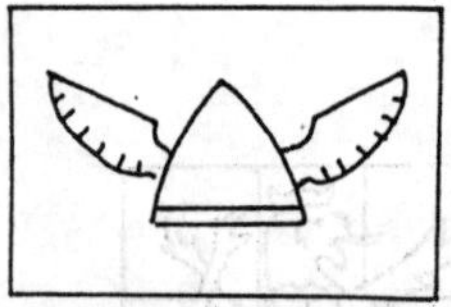

214th INFANTRY BRIGADE

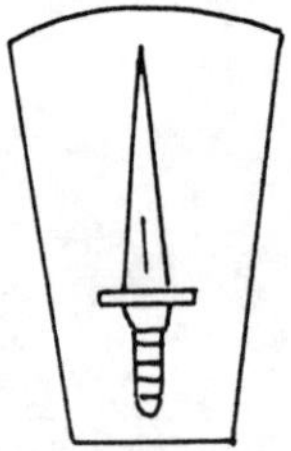

COMMANDO BRIGADES

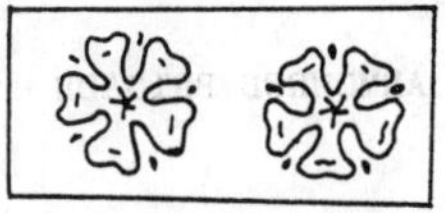

71st INFANTRY BRIGADE

COLOUR KEY TO INSIGNIA

21st ARMY GROUP*[1]
Red shield, blue cross, gold swords

L of C 21st ARMY GROUP*[2]
Yellow shield, blue cross

SECOND ARMY
White shield & sword, gold hilt, blue cross

FIRST CANADIAN ARMY
Gold maple leaf on red/black/red

I CORPS
White spearhead on red (black for vehicles)

VIII CORPS
White knight on red background

XII CORPS
Black, white oval, green foiliage & grass

XXX CORPS
White disc, black boar & background

CANADIAN CORPS
Gold leaf on red/white/red, red diamond (I Cdn Corps), blue diamond (II Cdn Corps)

AIR DESPATCH GROUP RASC
Yellow aircraft on royal blue

WAR DEPARTMENT FLEET RASC
Blue ensign with army swords

GHQ LIAISON REGIMENT
White 'P' on black

BEACH GROUPS
Red anchor & border on pale blue

AIR FORMATION SIGNALS
White wings & frame on blue

AIRFIELD CONSTRUCTION GROUPS RE
White bars on red-green-blue

1st & 6th AIRBORNE DIVISIONS
Pale blue motif on maroon

3rd INFANTRY DIVISION
Red triangle on black triangle

5th INFANTRY DIVISION
White 'Y' on khaki background

7th ARMOURED DIVISION
Red jerboa & square, white disc
(or red jerboa on white square)

11th ARMOURED DIVISION
Black bull, red nostrils, eyes,
horns, hooves, all on yellow

GUARDS ARMOURED DIVISION
White eye, blue shield, red edge

POLISH ARMOURED DIVISION
Black, yellow disc on khaki

15th INFANTRY DIVISION
Red lion, yellow disc, white
ring, black background

43rd INFANTRY DIVISION
Gold wyvern on blue background

49th INFANTRY DIVISION
White bear on black

50th INFANTRY DIVISION
Red 'T's on black background

51st INFANTRY DIVISION
Red motif on pale blue square

52nd INFANTRY DIVISION
White cross & title on blue

53rd INFANTRY DIVISION
Red 'W', green background

59th INFANTRY DIVISION
Red on blue, black background

79th ARMOURED DIVISION
Black/white head, red nostrils
& horn-tips, black frame all
on yellow triangle

CANADIAN DIVISIONS
Gold maple leaf on red (1 Div),
blue (2 Div), grey (3 Div),
green (4 ADiv), maroon (5 ADiv)

6th GUARDS TANK BRIGADE
Blue/red/blue bars, white
shield, gold sword

1st TANK BRIGADE
Red diablo

33rd ARMOURED BRIGADE
Green over black diablo

31st TANK BRIGADE
Light green Diablo

4th ARMOURED BRIGADE
Black jerboa on white

8th ARMOURED BRIGADE
Red-brown mask on yellow

27th ARMOURED BRIGADE
Gold seahorse, blue shield

34th TANK BRIGADE
White, yellow bar, red shield

PRINSES IRENE BRIGADE
Gold Netherlands lion

1st BELGIAN BRIGADE
Gold lion on black, red frame

CZEC ARMOURED BRIGADE
White lion, red cross on blue

1st CDN ARMOURED BRIGADE
Black/red/black with gold leaf
(also black/red/black diamond)

2nd CDN ARMOURED BRIGADE
Black/blue/black, gold leaf
(also black/blue/black diamond)

56th INFANTRY BRIGADE
Black disc, yellow sphinx and
background

71st INFANTRY BRIGADE
Red & white rose on black

214th INFANTRY BRIGADE
Red helmet on blue

231st INFANTRY BRIGADE
White cross on red shield

COMMANDO BRIGADES
Red dagger on black background

*[1] This insignia was adopted by British Army on the Rhine (BAOR) on formation, August 1945

*[2] This insignia adopted for HQ British Troops in the Low Countries from August 1945

BRITISH ARMY ON THE RHINE - 11th May 1946

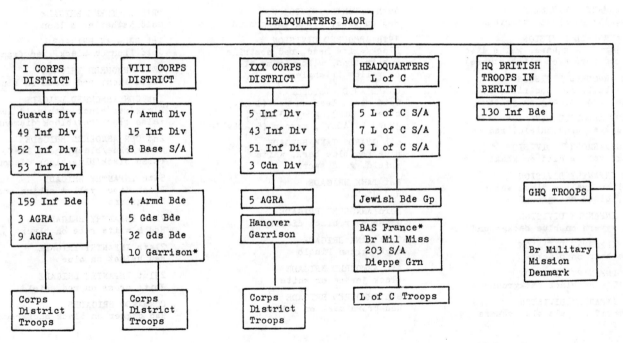

* Admin only

MAP SECTION

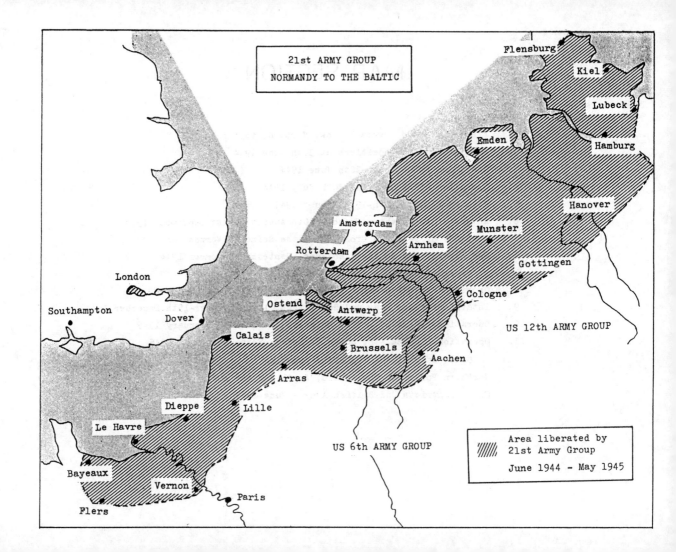

21st ARMY GROUP
NORMANDY TO THE BALTIC

Area liberated by
21st Army Group
June 1944 - May 1945

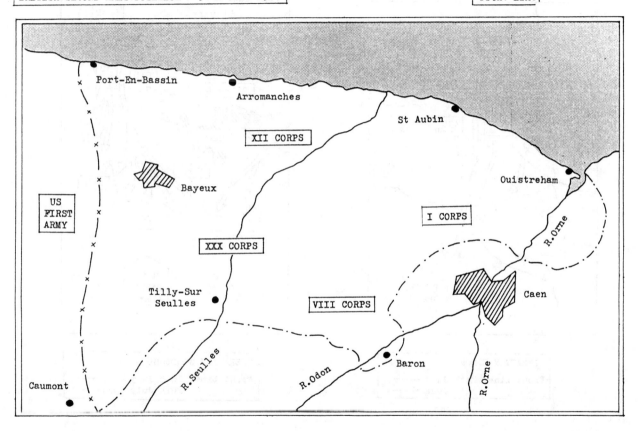

BRITISH SECOND ARMY POSITION - 30th JUNE 1944

Front Line — ·— ·—

US FIRST ARMY

Port-En-Bassin

Arromanches

St Aubin

XII CORPS

Bayeux

Ouistreham

I CORPS

R.Orne

XXX CORPS

Tilly-Sur Seulles

VIII CORPS

Caen

R.Seulles

R.Odon

Baron

R.Orne

Caumont

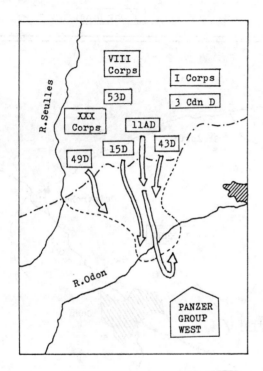

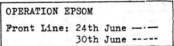

OPERATION EPSOM

Front Line: 24th June —·—
            30th June -----

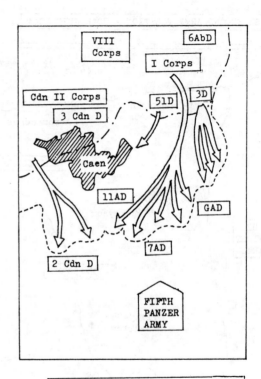

OPERATION GOODWOOD

Front Line: 18th July (am)—·—
            20th July (pm)-----

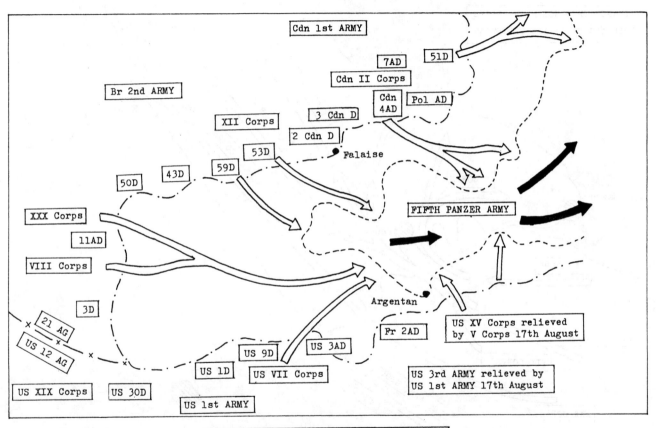

THE FALAISE POCKET - 16th to 21st AUGUST

Front Line: 16th August (pm) —·—·—
19th August (pm) ----

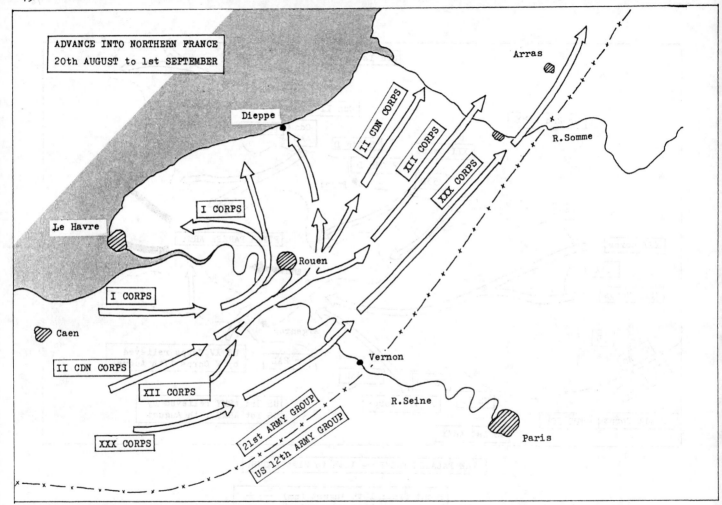

ADVANCE INTO NORTHERN FRANCE
20th AUGUST to 1st SEPTEMBER

Arras

R. Somme

Dieppe

II CDN CORPS

XII CORPS

XXX CORPS

I CORPS

Le Havre

I CORPS

Rouen

Caen

II CDN CORPS

XII CORPS

Vernon

R. Seine

XXX CORPS

21st ARMY GROUP

US 12th ARMY GROUP

Paris

ASSAULT CROSSING OF THE SEINE AT VERNON - 25th to 28th AUGUST 1944

43rd (WESSEX) INFANTRY DIVISION

HQ & Signals 43 Inf Div

43 Recce Regt RAC

8 Middlesex Regiment (MG)

Infantry:

129 Infantry Brigade
4 Somerset LI
4 Wiltshire Regt
5 Wiltshire Regt

130 Infantry Brigade
7 Hampshire Regt
4 Dorset Regt
5 Dorset Regt

214 Infantry Brigade
7 Somerset LI
1 Worcestershire Regt
5 Duke of Cornwalls LI

Ordnance:

43 Div Fld Park RAOC

Transport:

504,505,506,54 Coys RASC

129,130,214 Bde Wksps REME

Provost:

57 Provost Coy,
54 Fld Cash Office

Artillery:

94,112,179 Fld Regts RA
59 Anti-Tank Regt RA
110 LAA Regt RA

attached: 121 Medium Regt RA
71 LAA Regt RA
622 Sqn AOP AAC

Engineers:

43 Div Engrs
204,260,553 Fld Coys, 207 Fld Park Coy

attached:

XXX Corps Troops Engrs (incl. 11 Fld Coy RE)

7 Army Troops Engineers

15 (Kent) GHQ Troops RE
582,583,584 Coys RE

Armour (attached)

15/19 Hussars (from 11 Armd Div)
4/7 Dgn Guards   (from 8 Armd Bde)
Sherwood Yeomanry

Medical:

129 Fld Ambulance (+ 49 Fld Surgical Unit)
130,214 Fld Ambulance
14,15 Fld Dressing Stations
38 Fld Hygene Unit
306 Mobile Laundry & Bath

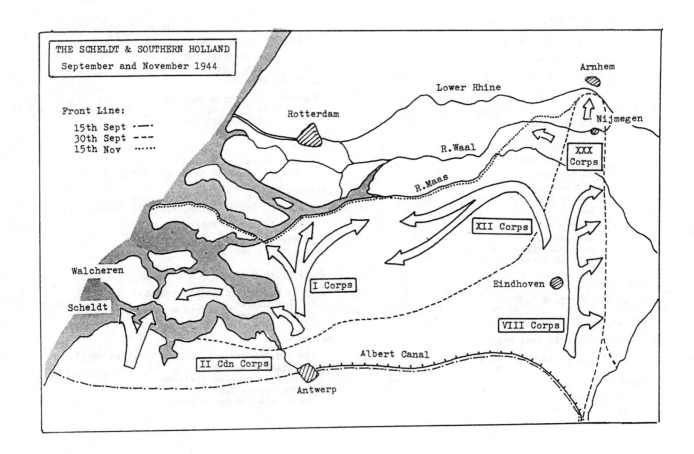

THE SCHELDT & SOUTHERN HOLLAND
September and November 1944

Front Line:
15th Sept ·—·
30th Sept ---
15th Nov ·····

Arnhem

Lower Rhine

Rotterdam

Nijmegen

R.Waal

XXX Corps

R.Maas

XII Corps

Walcheren

I Corps

Eindhoven

VIII Corps

Scheldt

II Cdn Corps

Albert Canal

Antwerp

THE SCHELDT ESTUARY - September/October 1944

Phase 1 : Breskens and the South of the Scheldt   Phase 2 : South Beveland from the East

Phase 3 : Seaborne Assault on Walcheren at Flushing   Phase 4 : Seaborne Assault on Walcheren at Westkapelle

BRITISH I CORPS & II CANADIAN CORPS

4th CDN ARMOURED DIVISION

  4th Cdn Armoured Brigade
  10th Cdn Infantry Brigade
   + British Colombia Regiment

1st POLISH ARMOURED DIVISION

  1st Polish Armoured Brigade
  3rd Polish Infantry Brigade
   + 10th Polish Dragoons

49th (WEST RIDING) DIVISION

  146th Infantry Brigade
  147th Infantry Brigade
  56th Infantry Brigade

52nd (LOWLAND) DIVISION

  155th Infantry Brigade
  156th Infantry Brigade
  157th Infantry Brigade

2nd CDN INFANTRY DIVISION

  4th Cdn Infantry Brigade
  5th Cdn Infantry Brigade
  6th Cdn Infantry Brigade

    8th Cdn Recce Regiment
    Toronto Scottish

3rd CDN INFANTRY DIVISION

  7th Cdn Infantry Brigade
   + 7 Cdn Recce Regt (Infantry)
   + 3 Anti-Tank Regt (Infantry)
  8th Cdn Infantry Brigade
  9th Cdn Infantry Brigade

4th COMMANDO BRIGADE

2nd CDN ARMOURED BRIGADE

141 REGT RAC (Sqn) - Crocodiles

NAVAL FORCE 'T'
SUPPORT SQN EASTERN FLANK
47th LANDING CRAFT FLOTILLA

ARTILLERY

4,5 & 6 Cdn Field Regts RCA
3,4 & 7 Cdn Med Regts RCA
2 Hvy AA Regiment RCA
452 Mtn Bty RA (3.7in)

ENGINEERS

8 & 9 Field Sqns RCE
16 Field Coy RCE
202 Field Coy RE

ARMOURED ASSAULT

79th ARMOURED DIVISION

  5th Assault Regiment RE
   (Buffaloes)
  82nd Assault Sqn RE
   (40x Terrapins)
  11 Royal Tank Regiment
   (Buffaloes)
  'B' Sqn Staffs Yeomanry
   (Sherman DD Tanks)
  1 Lothians (Crab Flails)

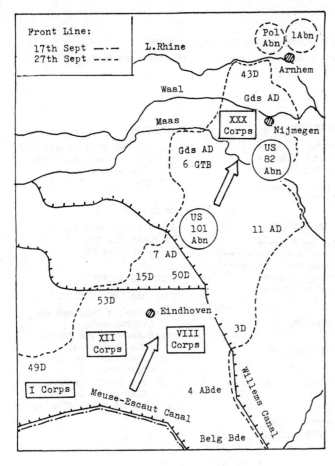

OPERATION MARKET GARDEN
September 17th-27th 1944

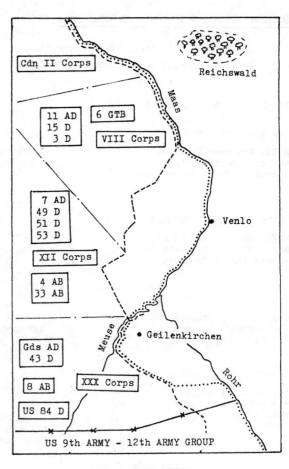

MAAS & ROHR LINES
14th Nov 1944 ---
15th Dec 1944 ·······

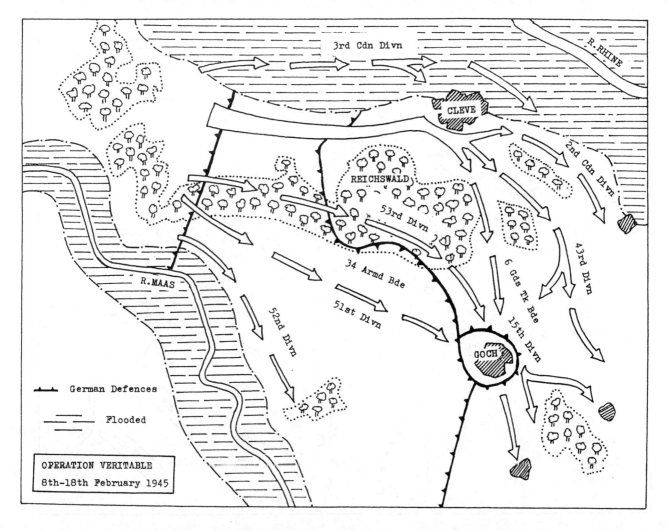

3rd Cdn Divn

R. RHINE

CLEVE

2nd Cdn Divn

REICHSWALD

53rd Divn

43rd Divn

34 Armd Bde

6 Gds Tk Bde

R. MAAS

52nd Divn

51st Divn

15th Divn

GOCH

▲ German Defences

Flooded

OPERATION VERITABLE
8th-18th February 1945

81

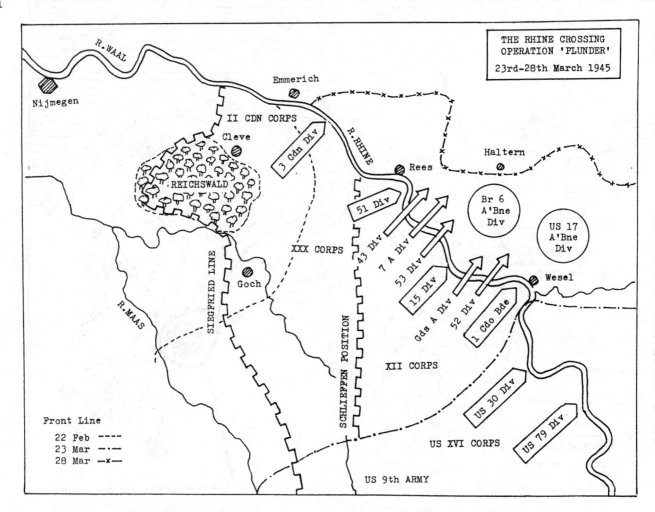

THE RHINE CROSSING
OPERATION 'PLUNDER'
23rd-28th March 1945

R.WAAL

Nijmegen

Emmerich

II CDN CORPS

Cleve

R.RHINE

Haltern

REICHSWALD

3 Cdn Div

51 Div

Rees

Br 6
A'Bne
Div

US 17
A'Bne
Div

XXX CORPS

43 Div

7 A Div

53 Div

Wesel

SIEGFRIED LINE

Goch

15 Div

Gds A Div

52 Div

1 Cdo Bde

R.MAAS

SCHLIEFFEN POSITION

XII CORPS

US 30 Div

US 79 Div

Front Line

22 Feb ----
23 Mar -·-·-
28 Mar -x-x-

US XVI CORPS

US 9th ARMY

THE RHINE CROSSING - 23rd to 28th March 1945

XII CORPS (ASSAULT)

15th (Scottish) Division (Assault)
1st Commando Brigade (Assault)

7th Armoured Division
52nd (Lowland) Division
53rd (Welsh) Division

4th Armoured Brigade
115th Infantry Brigade (part)
31st Armoured Brigade (part)
34th Armoured Brigade

3, 8 & 9 AGRA
100 AA Brigade RA

11 AGRE

11 Royal Tank Regiment (Buffalo)
East Riding Yeomanry (Buffalo)
77 Assault Sqn RE (Buffalo)
7 Royal Tank Regiment (Crocodile)
49 APC Regiment RAC (Kangaroo)
Westminster Dragoons (Crab Flails)
49 RTR (½ Sqn) (CDL)
44 Royal Tank Regiment (DD Tanks)
82 Assault Sqn RE (AVRE)
81, 16 & 222 Assault Sqns RE
  (Class 50/60 Rafts)

XXX CORPS (ASSAULT)

51st (Highland) Division (Assault)

Guards Armoured Division
3rd Infantry Division
3rd Cdn Infantry Division
43rd (Wessex) Division

8th Armoured Brigade
115th Infantry Brigade (part)
31st Armoured Brigade (part)

4 & 5 AGRA
106 AA Brigade RA

13 AGRE

4 Royal Tank Regiment (Buffalo)
1 Northants Yeomanry (Buffalo)
141 Regiment RAC (Crocodile)
Fife & Forfar Yeomanry (Crocodile)
1 Cdn APC Regt (Sqn) (Kangaroo)
22 Dragoons (Crab Flails)
49 RTR (½ Sqn)(CDL)
Staffs Yeomanry (DD Tanks)
26 Assault Sqn RE (AVRE)
79, 284 & 617 Assault Sqns RE
  (Class 50/60 Rafts)

XVIII US AIRBORNE CORPS (ASSAULT)

6th (Br) Airborne Division

17th (US) Airborne Division
  19th Glider Infantry Regiment
  507th Para Infantry Regiment
  513rd Para Infantry Regiment

II CDN CORPS (FOLLOW UP)

4th Cdn Armoured Division
2nd Cdn Infantry Division

2nd Cdn Armoured Brigade

2 Cdn AGRA
107th AA Brigade RA

VIII CORPS (ARMY RESERVE)

11th Armoured Division
6th Guards Armoured Brigade

ARMY TROOPS

10 AGRE, 12 AGRE (Airfields)

US XVI CORPS (attached units)

Fife & Forfar Yeomanry (one Sqn)
1 Lothian & Border Horse (one Sqn)
  (Crab Flails)

US 9th Army came under command 21st Army Group for Rhine Crossing: US XVI Corps (Assault) - 8AD,30D,35D,75D,79D ;
US XIX Corps (Follow-up) - 2AD,29D,83D,95D ; US XII Corps (Army Reserve) - 5AD,84D,102D ; Army Troops

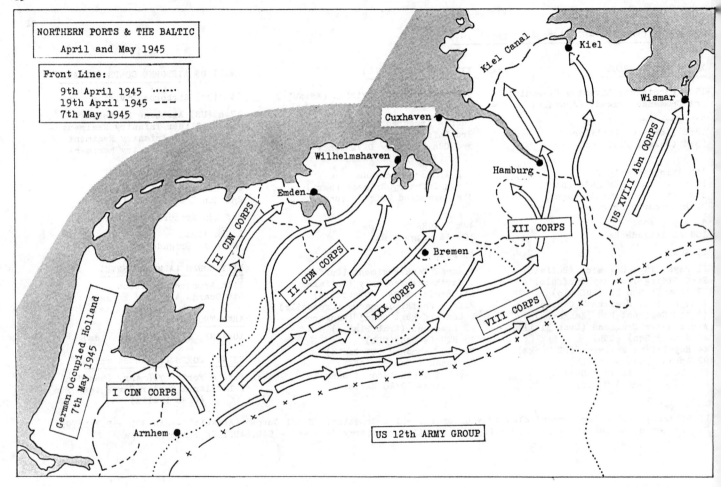

NORTHERN PORTS & THE BALTIC
April and May 1945

Front Line:
9th April 1945 ....
19th April 1945 -- -- --
7th May 1945 — — —

Kiel Canal

Kiel

Wismar

Cuxhaven

Wilhelmshaven

Emden

Hamburg

US XVIII Abn CORPS

II CDN CORPS

XII CORPS

II CDN CORPS

Bremen

XXX CORPS

VIII CORPS

German Occupied Holland
7th May 1945

I CDN CORPS

Arnhem

US 12th ARMY GROUP

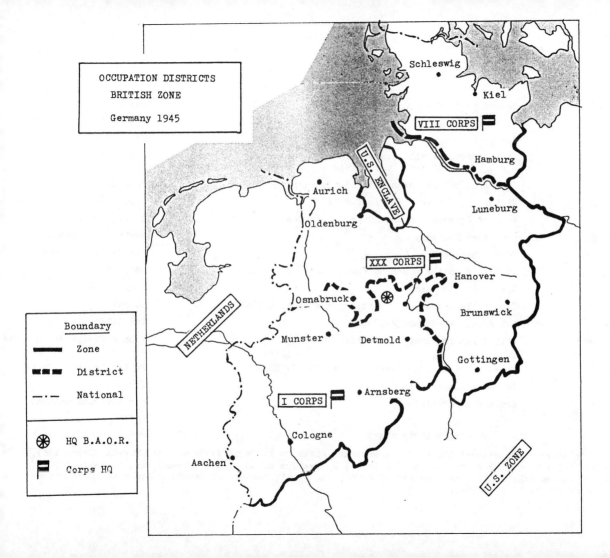

SELECT BIBLIOGRAPHY

Boileau, Col D.W.	Second World War - Supplies & Transport Vol II	War Office 1954
Cole, Lt Col H.N.	Formation Badges of World War Two	Arms & Armour Press
Crew, F.A.E.	The Army Medical Services - Campaigns Vol IV	HMSO 1962
Donnison, F.S.V.	Civil Affairs & Military Government - North West Europe 1944 - 1946	HMSO 1961
Duncan, N.	79th Armoured Division - Hobo's Funnies	Profile
Ellis, Major L.F.	Victory in The West - Vols I & II	HMSO 1962
Ford K.	Assault Crossing of the River Seine 1944	David & Charles
Hartcup G.	Code Name Mulberry	David & Charles
Horrocks, Gen Sir B.	Corps Commander	Sedgewick & Jackson
Joslen, Lt Col H.F.	Orders of Battle - Second World War Vols I & II	HMSO 1961
Keegan, J.	Six Armies in Normandy	Penguin 1983
Rawlings, G.	Cinderella Operation : Battle for Walcheren 1944	Cassell
Rowledge, J.P.W.	Austerity 2-8-0s and 2-10-0s	Ian Allen
US Division of Naval Intelligence	Allied Landing Craft and Ships	Pubn & Distbn Branch 1944
War Ministry	Files, various, PRO Class WO 171, WO 32/16618	Public Records Office
Weekes, J.	The Airborne Soldier	Blandford
Wynn H. & Young S.	Prelude to Overlord	Airlife Publications

ACKNOWLEDGEMENTS

The author wishes to express his sincere thanks for assistance given by Mr David Fletcher (RAC Museum, Bovington), Mr Stephen Brookes (D-Day Museum, Portsmouth), Lt Col (retd) R. Eyeions O.B.E. (RAMC Museum), Mr. P. Poole B.E.M., (RADC Museum), Mrs Maureen Bellis BEd Hons, Members of MAFVA, and to all readers of Datafile Books who have given Support and encouragement to this venture.

THE DATAFILE SERIES

DATAFILE 1 (2nd Edition)
'British Tanks & Formations 1939-45'
ISBN 0 9512126 2 1

DATAFILE 2
'Divisions of the British Army 1939-45'
ISBN 0 9512126 0 5

DATAFILE 3
'Brigades of the British Army 1939-45'
ISBN 0 9512126 1 3

DATAFILE 4
'German Tanks & Formations 1939-45'
ISBN 0 9512126 4 8

DATAFILE 5
'British Armoured & Infantry Regiments
1939-45'
ISBN 0 9512126 3 X

DATAFILE 6
'U.S. Divisions - N.Africa & Europe 1942-45'
ISBN 0 9512126 5 6

DATAFILE 7
'U.S. Tank Destroyers of World War Two'
ISBN 0 9512126 6 4